PHONICS THAT WORK!

New Strategies for
the Reading/Writing Classroom

By Janiel M. Wagstaff

SCHOLASTIC
PROFESSIONAL BOOKS

NEW YORK • TORONTO • LONDON • AUCKLAND • SYDNEY

This book is dedicated to the children who helped me learn the lessons it contains. My hope is that special teachers will benefit from its use, as will those under their careful guidance.

Acknowledgements
Special thanks goes to Marilyn Jager Adams, whose extensive review of reading research led me to discover a new way to help children work with words. Thanks also to my friends and colleagues at the University of Utah, including Emily Anderson, Kathleen Brown, Jan Dole, Ralph Reynolds, and Gale Sinatra. Additional appreciation goes to Lynn Champagne and Barb Jansz, two wonderful teachers, whose feedback has been invaluable.

I am grateful for husband, John, and my family, whose guidance and support has fueled my thinking. Lastly, thanks to the developers of The Benchmark Program, and particularly, Patricia Cunningham, who have led the way in bringing analogy instruction into our schools.

"Boa Constrictor" from WHERE THE SIDEWALK ENDS by Shel Silverstein. Copyright © 1974 by Evil Eye Music, Inc. Reprinted by permission of HarperCollins Children's Books, a division of HarperCollins Publishers Inc.

To contact the Benchmark program, write:
The Benchmark School
2107 North Providence Road
Media, PA 19063

Conceptualizations for this book were based on the article, "Promoting Efficient and Independent Word Recognition: A New Strategy for Readers and Writers." Wagstaff, J.M. & Sinatra, G.M. (in preparation).

Cover design by Vincent Ceci
Interior design by Joan Gazdik Gillner
Illustration by Arnie Ten
Production by Judith A.V. Harlan

ISBN 0-590-49624-7

TABLE OF CONTENTS

■ Chapter 5: Student Progress 67

■ Chapter 6: Reflections 97

Introduction

I wrote this book because I want to help improve the way reading and writing is taught in our schools. My first years of teaching second graders to read and write were unsatisfying. I was using traditional methods, but they didn't seem to promote much progress for the majority of my students. I was upset that I was unable to help those students who needed me. Perhaps you have felt the same way.

I have since found out why my old methods were not working. I have also discovered new strategies for teaching reading and writing that correct the old mistakes. These strategies make sense and really work for learners. They can be taught in integrated, purposeful ways within classrooms where rich, authentic reading and writing experiences are top priority. The whole language movement has done much to set our drill-oriented tradition on its ear. I believe that quality time spent on real reading and real writing is the key to a successful and joyful literacy program. Thus, I have worked these new strategies into a very exciting literacy program that is consistent with recent findings about how children develop and best learn.

These strategies help students use different cues within the contexts of enjoying literature and creating their own stories. The new strategies offered here improve the way phonics can be used as an effective reading and writing tool within integrated language arts programs.

When students are able successfully to use all cues available to them as readers and writers, they make amazing gains; I've seen it in my own students' progress. The

> *T*his book is not about "old phonics"! It offers something new. Students are not taught confusing rules or drilled on unreliable letter-sounds. They do not engage in purposeless activities devoid of functional connections to real reading and writing processes. Instead they are taught helpful, effective strategies that complement our current focus on meaning and structure cues in texts.

strategies have proven to be beneficial to all learners, even those who were really struggling. They have provided better access to reading and writing for my advanced students as well. Even I have benefited. As a poor speller, I have noticed how my understanding of the strategies has changed the way I tackle spelling problems.

If you want your students to be more independent, if you believe in using literature and writing to promote growth, if you strive to provide balanced instruction that fits the needs of all learners, and if you wish to offer all your students strategies to help them as readers and writers, this book is for you. It is with confidence and excitement that I share these new strategies. I hope by reading this book you will share my enthusiasm and will then incorporate the instruction into your language arts program. I know your students will find these strategies helpful and will greatly benefit from their use.

A Journey toward Change

As a beginning teacher, the materials I used to teach reading and writing consisted of a basal text, student workbooks, the accompanying teacher's guide, and a number of skill-building ditto worksheets I had purchased at a local teachers' store. From these resources, I taught reading and writing. Looking back on it now, I realize that I was teaching isolated skills that did not result in useful strategies for developing readers and writers. At the time, however, I felt that if I did my job well using these methods and teaching these skills, I would help children learn to read and write. I soon found out I was wrong.

My reading lessons followed a contrived set of activities: vocabulary for the basal story, reading the story with students, and asking questions from the teaching manual. The students did the corresponding workbook pages.

Our writing curriculum was reduced to learning grammatical conventions, filling in blanks, or writing a sentence or two. The classroom took on an assembly line atmosphere, with students filling in worksheets and recording numerical scores. I had always loved children's literature and creative writing, but there seemed to be little time to devote to these activities. Students were not developing a love for books and stories. Moreover, when I did make time for creative writing, students did not use the skills they had been taught.

I was teaching what I was told to teach; they were learning what they were told to learn. Day after day, our motions were guided by the fine print in the teacher's manual. It was a safe method, full of structure, free of risk. But it was a joyless process for all of us.

■ Is Drill Instruction Useful?

As a second-grade teacher, I soon realized that my teacher's manual was not providing me with methods for helping students who were struggling with reading. I hoped that phonics instruction would help bring them along, so I taught phonetic "rules," like "When two vowels go walking, the first one does the talking." We worked on letter-sound correspondences, and the students practiced with their phonics workbooks. Unfortunately, our phonics lessons, which focused on decoding individual letter sounds, then blending the sounds together to make words, seemed useless. Students either could not remember the rules or could not make enough sense of them to apply the rules when reading.

> *Little did I know that the rules I was teaching were not reliable and that many of the letter-sound correspondences I had taught through phonics were unreliable, too, because their sounds were so variable. I only knew that what I was teaching wasn't helping students learn to read.*

I remained determined to devote more time to real reading and writing. I attended local language arts conferences and continued my education. As I examined relevant research, it became clear that my teaching of skills had been artificial. Skills and strategies taught only through drill and practice do not transfer easily to more meaningful reading and writing situations (Collins, Brown, & Newman, 1989). My worksheet-based methods emphasized conventions only and demonstrated skills to students in a manner that was detached from real composing and not true to life. Of course, students were unable to apply to their writing the skills they had been taught.

The same was true of my reading instruction. I taught in isolated, artificial ways the skills and strategies I wanted my students to use as readers. But reading, like writing, is a complex process, in which a number of different factors such as phonics, syntax (i.e., word order), semantics (meaning), comprehension, and background knowledge all come into play. How could my students possibly take what they had learned in an isolated exercise and apply it to the real act of reading? I needed to teach skills and strategies in the context of their use—and I could only accomplish that by engaging students in real reading and writing.

■ More Holistic Instruction: Teaching with Real Reading and Writing

As I learned about reading and writing workshops, I set aside the rote methods and began investing in more children's literature. I devoted substantial time to shared reading with big books, guided reading with multiple copies of trade books, and independent reading. Students and I discussed books in meaningful ways and kept literature logs in which we dialogued back and forth about our reading. Students chose what they would read and write, and I tried to address their individual needs over the curriculum guidelines.

The focus of my lessons changed from teaching skills directly to modeling strategies. I encouraged students to make hypotheses about unknown words in texts, and they learned to use the beginning sounds of words coupled with the meaning of text to solve decoding problems. I began to feel more confident about my language arts teaching because these methods seemed to help students apply their learning.

I made similar changes in my writing instruction. I modeled the writing process (Nancy Atwell, 1987) for my students and developed my own methods for teaching writing in context. My students imitated what I was doing because they wanted to be involved in the fun of purposeful communication.

My life as a teacher changed. The joy and excitement was back; I could feel it and so could the students. Progress was much more readily apparent than with my previous drill instruction. Students were now using the strategies and skills used by real writers that had been demonstrated in context.

> *An onset is the portion of a syllable that precedes the vowel. In the word* church, *the onset is* ch. *A rime is the portion of the syllable including the vowel(s) and any consonant(s) that follow. In* church, *the rime is* urch. *Not all syllables or words have onsets, but they all have a rime. For example, the word or syllable* out *is a rime without an onset.*

■ The Need for Independent, Efficient Strategies

Still, something troubled me. I liked the fact that my classroom had become a community of learners, but students' asking neighbors for help with unknown words and proper spellings was taking time and attention away from comprehending or composing text. Wasn't this the same problem I had observed before, when students were struggling to decode words during reading group or to encode words during writing?

I began to wonder about some of the other strategies I had been teaching. I observed that strategies such as predicting the unknown words based on context and beginning sounds, reading on in the passage to clarify meaning, rereading parts of the text, and calling up background knowledge were successful only part of the time. When they didn't work, we would tackle the problem head on and rely on all the graphophonic cues in the words. We were then back where we had started: letter-by-letter decoding and individual sound-symbol relationships! There had to be something more, something faster and more reliable that would preserve meaning better than the strategies I was teaching. I found it during a graduate school reading seminar.

During the course of my reading for the seminar, I learned that my basic intuition about phonics (that some type of phonics instruction is necessary in the primary grades) was correct. Readers rely on three cuing systems in combination while reading. These are syntax, semantics, and graphophonics (Hearst & Burke, 1977). Responsible educators cannot emphasize the former two while ignoring the latter or teaching it through poor methods.

Marilyn Jager Adams (1990) summarizes research that unequivocally proves the important role of phonics in learning to read: "The best differentiator between good and poor readers is repeatedly found to be their knowledge of spelling patterns and their proficiency with spelling-sound translations." We need to provide students with help—but we need a new type of phonics that works.

■ Onset and Rime: A New Focus for Readers and Writers

Even when taught in context through effective techniques, individual letter-sound correspondences are highly unreliable. Individual letters, especially vowels, make different sounds depending on the syllables they are embedded in. This is because the sounds that letters make often depend on the letters that surround them. The syllable itself, and the parts within it, are therefore more reliable than individual letter-sounds, producing more consistent sounds across different words. So it may be more effective for readers to focus on a portion of the word that is bigger than individual phonemes (letter-sound correspondences).

These larger units, called *onsets* and *rimes,* are intersyllabic units that are smaller than words and syllables but larger than phonemes. An onset is the portion of a syllable that precedes the vowel. In the word *church,* the onset is *ch.* A rime is the portion of the syllable including the vowel(s) and any consonant(s) that follow. In *church,* the rime is *urch.* Not all syllables or words have onsets, but they all have a rime. For example, the word or syllable *out* is a rime without an onset. In multisyllabic words, the syllables may be split in the same way. In the word *helicopter, h, c,* and *t* are simple onsets, while *el, i, op,* and *er* are the rimes in each syllable.

Adams contends that the path of phonological awareness, or the way in which learners become aware of sounds and symbols, proceeds from larger units to smaller units. So, learners can recognize and manipulate sentences before words, words before syllables, and syllables before phonemes. Because onsets and rimes are larger units than phonemes, they should be easier to use and attend to than phonemes. It was little wonder that the instruction I had been giving, which focused on individual letters and sounds, provided minimal help for my readers and writers.

I wanted to find out more about these mysterious units. Why hadn't I ever heard of onset and rime before? What made the researchers so sure these units really existed and were the focus of readers' attention? How did they work? Would onset and rime help my students become more independent readers and writers?

Adams, M. J. (1990). *Beginning to read: Thinking and learning about print.* Cambridge, MA: MIT Press.

Atwell, N. (1987). *In the middle: Writing, reading, and learning with adolescents.* Upper Montclair, NJ: Boyton/Cook.

Collins, A., Brown J.S., & Newman, S.E. (1989) Cognitive apprenticeship: Teaching the crafts of reading, writing, and mathematics. In L.B. Resnick (Ed.). *Knowing, learning, & instruction: Essays in honor of Robert Glaser (pp. 453-494). Hillsdale, NJ: LEA*

Harste, J.C., &C.L. Burke. (1977). A new hypothesis for reading teacher research: Both teaching and learning of reading are theoretically based. In P.D. Pearson and J. Hansen (Eds.) *Reading: Theory, research, and practice, Twenty Sixth Yearbook of the National Reading Conference.* Clemson, SC: National Reading Conference. ED 227 440.

RESEARCH
LAB

A New Look at Old Phonics

■ A Review of the Research

In presenting evidence for the existence of onset and rime, Adams explains that many researchers have questioned why children commonly can decipher individual consonant sounds if they come at the beginning of a word but have trouble decoding the same sound if it falls at the end of a word. To cite Adams's example, "if the child knows that *p* says |p| in *pat,* why would she or he fail to realize that it said |p| in *tap?*" The conclusion is that *p* in *pat* is easier to decode because it is the whole onset of the word, whereas *p* in *tap* is harder to decode because it is an integral part of the rime *ap* and, as such, cannot be easily stripped away from the whole unit to produce an individual sound. It is harder for the child to decode the *p* in *tap* because to do so requires awareness at the more developmentally complex phoneme level.

A study done by Liberman (1973) showed that children make

more errors in reading vowel sounds than consonant sounds. In one experiment, when children were asked to tap out phonemes in a syllable, they were more likely to miss the vowel than the consonant sounds. When asked to tap out each sound in the word *cat,* for instance, a typical error would be to identify |c| as a sound and |at| as a sound, not |c| |a| |t|.

> *A* study done by Liberman (1973) showed that children make more errors in reading vowel sounds than consonant sounds.

Researchers conclude that it is difficult to isolate vowel sounds because the vowel(s) and subsequent consonant(s) work together to form a whole rime. Again, this unit is hard to dissect, making the vowel sound more difficult to identify on its own.

Other studies show similar evidence that onset and rime exist and that, in fact, it is easier for children to read whole rimes than individual phonemes. In a study by Treiman (1985), subjects were asked to read nonwords made up of the same letters, like *smoo* and *soom.* The researcher argued that if the first- and second-grade students attended to individual phonemes with ease, they would read the word pairs with equal accuracy because they are composed of the same letters. In fact, the students made more errors with nonwords like *smoo* than with nonwords like *soom.* Why? Because of the more complex nature of the onset in *smoo*—a consonant cluster as opposed to the single consonant onset in *soom.* This and other studies (Goswami, 1988) suggest that students find the whole onset and rime units easier to use in decoding.

Adams corroborates this evidence with another study done by Wylie and Durrell (1970). In this study, subjects were shown rimes like *ack* and *ock.* In one group, children were asked to identify a whole rime from a series of choices. In another group, children were asked to identify individual vowel sounds from a series of rime choices. Subjects were much more successful at identifying the whole rimes than individual vowel sounds. These findings suggest, again, that onset and rime exist and are exploited by beginning readers with less effort than phonemes.

One more area of information in Adams's book intrigued me. This is evidence from errors in speech, word abbreviations, and strangely enough, pig Latin.

Common errors in speech involve mispronunciations of words wherein whole units are jumbled, but the onset and rime remain intact. For instance, when *butterfly* is mistakenly said as *flutterby,* the rimes remain unaffected. Onsets and rimes are not commonly broken up or dissected into parts in these errors in speech.

The above example demonstrates that onsets and rimes behave as units. The same can be seen in the way we create word abbreviations. We commonly use whole onsets for abbreviations, as in *Fr.* for *France* or *Sp.* for *Spain.*

And what about pig Latin? Consider the construction *ick-stay* for the word *stick.* The *ay* is added (note that this addition is a whole rime), while the onset is stripped away from the rime and their order is reversed.

Subjects were much more successful at identifying the whole rimes than individual vowel sounds. These findings suggest, again, that onset and rime exist and are exploited by beginning readers with less effort than phonemes.

All of these findings converge to suggest that onset and rime are real units of words and that they may be easier for developing readers to use than individual phonemes. Yet, there is more. Onset and rime provide logical answers to other problems that plague beginning readers.

■ Why Traditional Phonics Rules Fail Readers and Writers

In isolation, the same vowels make many different sounds and can pose real problems for developing readers. That may be why we've taught students so many rules for dealing with vowels. Adams tackles the unreliable nature of vowel sounds and the unhelpful rules we teach to help readers decode them by including a table based on Theodore Clymer's study (1963) of the utility of phonic generalizations.

got
hot
not
pot
spot
dot
et
get
let
met
pet
net
jet
set
wet
un
sun
run
fun
bun
gun

Remember the rule "When two vowels go *walking,* the first one does the *talking* and says its own name"? Clymer found 309 cases in his study in which this was true, and 377 where it was false. In other words, the rule was useful only 45 percent of the time. Other rules fared much worse, including one generalization about words ending with *y* or *ey,* which was effective zero percent of the time. Clymer concludes, "In evaluating this initial venture in testing the utility of phonic generalizations, it seems quite clear that many generalizations which are commonly taught are of limited value." (255) What an understatement!

■ How Rimes Can Help

Rimes are consistent and reliable, while vowel sounds and rules are not. In fact, Wylie and Durrell found that the vowels contained in a list of 286 rimes from primary grade texts were pronounced the same way 95 percent of the time. Additionally, these researchers show how only 37 rimes make up approximately 500 primary grade words. These common rimes are (Adams, 1990, 321-322):

ack	ank	eat	ill	ock	ump
ail	ap	ell	in	oke	unk
ain	ash	est	ine	op	
ake	at	ice	ing	ore	
ale	ate	ick	ink	uck	
ame	aw	ide	ip	ug	
an	ay	ight	it		

Rimes seem to provide the basis for easier vowel learning because the letters that follow the vowel(s) seem to influence the sound(s) the vowel(s) makes. Wylie and Durell provide support for this theory by demonstrating how children easily learn rimes, even those that contain "irregular" vowels that we normally call special attention to in our classrooms (like r-controlled vowels).

But, if the individual letter sounds are so variable, letter-by-letter decoding doesn't work, and the old rules are not truly helpful, how have so many of us learned to read through these methods?

Some students become adept at reading by making sense of the code in their own way from extensive reading and writing experience. Others may rely more heavily on other cues initially to gain fluency in reading, although they may ultimately lack helpful phonetic strategies. Then, of course, there are many students who continue to struggle to read throughout their entire school experience. Some never master the code.

Attention to onset and rime provides students with more reliable phonetic cues. These cues assist students in breaking the code faster and more easily than did our old methods.

■ Analogy Strategies: What They Are and How They Work

The fact is, fluent readers don't readily use the strategies we offer to developing readers. When you decode the nonsense word *sanditerous,* for example, do you focus on each individual letter, trying to associate an isolated sound for each grapheme? Then, do you try to blend these distinct sounds together? If you do, your thought processes might go something like this, "|s| and |a| make |sa|, |n| and |d| combine with |sa| to produce |sand|, |i| |t| …now is that the short *i* or the long *i* sound?" Do you call upon rules to determine the vowel sound? Probably not. You would probably use different strategies entirely. You may have devoted your attention to the chunks in the nonsense word. You may have recognized *sand* and *it, er* and *ous* as whole parts, then put them together to create a word. The specific strategy you may have used, and which I now teach my students, is called *decoding by analogy*.

Decoding by analogy was first described by Patricia Cunningham (1975–76). When readers encounter unknown words, they are likely to attend to the patterns in these words. Using their knowledge of other words with identical patterns, they may decode these chunks. Putting these sounds together provides the whole word. This process is more reliable than letter-by-letter decoding, and it eliminates the need for blending each sound. Decoding by analogy is what makes onset and rime useful to readers.

In decoding our nonsense word, you automatically recognized common rimes or spelling patterns (or in the case of *sand,* you easily recognized the whole syllable), and knew the sounds associated with them based on your familiarity with these patterns in other real words. You knew the sounds of the chunks without difficulty because the rimes are common, consistent, and reliable. However, if the word contained an unfamiliar rime, you could have called to mind another word containing the same pattern, thereby decoding by analogy.

The human brain works as a "pattern detector" (Cunningham, 1992). When we encounter an unknown word, we search our memory stores for a word with a matching pattern. Second graders may not have automatically recognized the rime *ous* because it is less frequent than the other rimes contained in the nonsense word. But, if second graders knew or could refer to the real word *fabulous,* for example, they could decode the last chunk by analogy to the known word, thinking, "I know |fab| |u| |lous|, so this must be |sand| |it| |er| |ous|."

Considering the path of phonological awareness/the nature of rimes—efficient, reliable, and accessible/and the strategies that adult fluent readers use, I was convinced that I had found the solution to the puzzle. Onset and rime could be the keys to providing my students with helpful strategies for making use of all the cues available to them as readers.

■ Making Onset and Rime Useful to Readers

I had a theory, but I was lacking a method for putting that theory into practice. I wondered, "How can I fit onset and rime into my daily instruction?" That's where the Benchmark Word Identification Program (1986) came in.

I am forever indebted to the developers of this program, Marjorie A. Downer, Irene W. Gaskins, and their colleagues, for providing me with the impetus to get started with these ideas in my classroom. I have since been helped by Patricia Cunningham's book, *Phonics They Use: Words for Reading and Writing* (1991) in making additions to my program.

The Benchmark School in Pennsylvania teamed up Richard C. Anderson and Patricia M. Cunningham at the Center for the Study of Reading in Illinois to devise a program that incorporated onset and rime into basic reading instruction. The Gaskins wanted to find a way to reach students who had failed as readers in traditional programs. They believed that the decoding by analogy strategy was the key to helping their students. They wanted to both immerse students in real books and in helpful instruction in decoding. Automaticity in decoding and an understanding of how the English sound system works were what their students lacked (Gaskins, et al., 1991).

Looking at their program, it became clear to me that decoding by analogy is the strategy that makes onset and rime useful. If I drilled students on the chunks without making real connections to reading and writing, I would be back to the old problem of decontextualized learning that lacks purpose. The strategy itself, which facilitates both reading and writing, is the answer to how onset and rime can be taught with purpose and could be helpful to students.

My job became showing students how to use the decoding by analogy strategy as readers and writers, and providing them with word references and familiarity with patterns from which to make analogies. Familiarity with patterns promotes automaticity in decoding. Gaskins et al. (1991) attest to the importance of automaticity: "We learned, as we had suspected, that automaticity in decoding words independent of context is characteristic of good readers, though not of poor readers." (214) Once students learn rime patterns and can freely use the strategy of decoding by analogy, the process becomes much quicker, requiring less mental processing and attention. In this way, the focus of the reader is devoted to comprehending text. This is always our main goal.

Students can apply the analogy strategy to writing in much the same way. As writers come to words they cannot automatically spell, they can listen for the onset and rime chunks in the words, and invent spellings by calling to mind or referring to words with like-sounding chunks. These invented spellings may not always be correct, but they will be closer to the intended words than invented spellings based on other strategies.

My students now have a spelling strategy that makes sense to them and is quicker and easier for them to use. Their confidence has increased dramatically. They are willing to attempt to spell anything, knowing the result will be close enough to make their messages clear to readers.

■ Introducing Analogy Minilessons

The next chapter explores analogy mini-lessons in depth. You will notice that the lessons are divided into two major strands: lessons that help students understand and apply the strategies in text, and lessons designed to help students develop familiarity and, ultimately, automaticity with patterns.

Because automatic decoding is key to freeing up mental capacity for comprehension and higher processes, I devote some review time to patterns. The analogy strategies in combination with pattern automaticity contribute to the great gains my students have made. You may, of course, decide to devote your time differently, depending on the unique needs of your students.

Clymer, T. (1963). The utility of phonic generalizations in the primary grades. *The Reading Teacher,* 16, 252-258.

Cunningham, P. M. 1975-76). Investigating a synthesized theory of mediated word identification. *Reading Research Quarterly,* 11, 127-143.

Cunningham, P.M. (1992). What kind of phonics instruction will we have? In C.K.Kinzer and D.J. Leu (Eds.) *Literacy reserch, theory, and practice: Views from many perspectives, Forty First Yearbook of the National Reading Conference.* (pp. 17-31). Chicago, IL: National Reading Conference, Inc.

Downer, M.A., & Gaskins, I.W. (1986) *Benchmark word identification/vocabulary development program.* Media, PA: Benchmark Press.

Gaskins, R.W., Gaskins, J.C., & Gaskins, I.W. (1991). A decoding program for poor readers—and the rest of the class, too! *Language Arts,* 68, 213-225.

Goswami, U. (1988). Orthographic analogies and reading development. *Quarterly Journal of Experimental Psychology.*

Liberman, I.Y. (1973). Segmentation of the spoken word and reading acquisition. *Bulletin of the Orton Society,* 23, 65-77.

Treiman, R. (1985). Onsets and rimes as units of spoken syllables: Evidence from children. *Journal of Experimental Child Psychology,* 39, 161-181.

Wylie, R.E., & Durrell, D.D. (1970). *Elementary English,* 47, 787-791.

Analogy Minilessons

I will share the lessons themselves before showing you how I integrate them into our daily schedule. This will provide you with a solid background from which to view the lessons within the entire context of an authentic reading and writing program. The activities vary to meet a range of abilities and learning styles of different students. Some involve review and explicit strategy teaching for students who benefit most from such instruction. Additionally, activities are multisensory. Students go beyond just visual learning when they write, chanting and clapping words and patterns. This variety assures that learning opportunities are maximized for all students.

There are three important points.

- First, the Analogy Minilessons are highly interactive. The fast-paced, cooperative interaction inherent in the activities makes them more successful and enjoyable for students and their teachers. **A cooperative community is built and maintained**

as interactive learning continues throughout the year.

- Second, as you read about the Analogy Minilessons, you will notice that interaction with students involves taking risks. Students make mistakes as they call out words they think are analogous to the key words during chant and check and practice pages, as they do when analogy is used to spell inventively. Of course, they also make mistakes while engaged in the processes of real reading and writing. These errors must be viewed as natural parts of the course of development. All mistakes are a welcome part of learning, and they are analyzed for the lessons they contain. If we examine what does *not* work, we are closer to finding what *does* work. I encourage students to share their errors, and I praise them for doing so while demanding respect for each other as learners. I often ask students if I may point out their mistake to the class, whether it is an error in spelling, math, or art, because it is a rich learning opportunity for all of us. My request is rarely turned down because of the nurturing learning environment present in our classroom. Students are well aware that I am the biggest mistake maker in the group. **I always share my errors with them, and help them see how we can learn from my example.**

- Finally, children at the kindergarten and first-grade levels should have the chance to enjoy stories and approximate reading and writing behaviors while immersed in rich experiences with language. A basic level of phonemic awareness is required, including knowledge of rhyming words and some knowledge of print, like letter names and consonant sounds, before students are ready to focus at the onset and rime level. However, this does not mean they must be taught all sounds before working with patterns. Rather, they acquire such knowledge as they participate in a variety of activities. Patricia Cunningham's book (1991) has several ideas for developing this type of phonological awareness and working with patterns. Her book contains many activities appropriate for grade one, and she has written articles about instruction, specifically at the first-grade level. If you are a first-grade teacher, I highly recommend her work to further your understanding of appropriate instruction geared to that level. Her "Making Words" lessons (1992) seem particularly good for first graders, as they guide inventive spellings, help students attend to patterns, and build phonemic knowledge. **Regardless of the grade you teach, you must consider the needs and abilities of your students as you work analogy into your daily schedule.**

■　　■　　■　　■　　■

Word Wall Selection. This is the first analogy minilesson of the school week. The Word Wall is an idea developed by Patricia Cunningham (1991). It involves selecting the words to be used as references for readers and writers. I choose our Word Wall words from favorite poems to capitalize on the fun language and on the intrinsic enjoyment my students have for poetry. I have always enjoyed incorporating the humorous poetry of Shel Silverstein and Jack Prelutsky into classroom activities.

> *The Word Wall may be used to accomplish different goals. We fill our Wall with key words for developing familiarity with rime patterns and for analogy use in reading and writing.*

Each week, we choose one poem, which we call our "New Favorite." I write the poem down and provide students with a copy on the first day of the week. We read the poem chorally, experimenting with different plans for reading. Then, we discuss the meaning and literary elements in the poem, and entertain student questions or comments before searching for words to place on our Word Wall.

The Benchmark Program has beginning, intermediate, and advanced lists with key words containing common spelling patterns. These lists may be used to guide key word choices. Each week, five words with useful spelling patterns are selected from the poem as our "Word of the Week." I began the year by using the intermediate list as a personal reference for common patterns. However, the list became unnecessary because it is easy to discern which words have spelling patterns that will be helpful to students without the use of such references. If you can find multiple words in your memory to fit a rime or spelling pattern within the chosen key word, you can bet the pattern will be useful to your students. Also, you can keep a list of words that are misread by your students when you observe them read. These commonly missed words may have patterns unfamiliar to your students.

After we choose five words with common patterns, they are written on cards. These cards are left on the front chalk tray for further use during the week.

Each year, my students and I include the poem "Boa Constrictor" by Shel Silverstein in our repertoire of favorites. Let's use this poem as an example of the "Word Wall Selection" minilesson.

Boa Constructor

Oh, I'm being eaten
By a boa constrictor,
A boa constrictor,
A boa constrictor,
I'm being eaten by a boa constrictor,
And I don't like it—-one bit.
Well, what do you know?
It's nibblin' my toe.
Oh, gee,
It's up to my knee.
Oh my,
It's up to my thigh.
Oh, fiddle,
It's up to my middle.
Oh, heck,
It's up to my neck.
Oh, dread,
It's upmmmmmmmmmffffffffff...

First I distribute copies of the poem to students. I leave space at the bottom for students to illustrate the poem if they choose. A variation of this is to write the poem on an overhead so all students have visual access to it.

Then we enjoy the poem orally. With their copies, they come to the front rug and begin reading with partners or on their own.

Students are given time to finish their own reading before we read together as a class.

Next, we read together chorally, having fun reading the poem. Then, students work with one another to explore ways of reading the poem that make use of varied voice patterns. For example, a plan may be for one half of the class to read the first line and the other half to read the second line, continuing the pattern throughout the reading of the poem. Partners share their ideas with the class, and we pick a few to try. During these repeated rereadings, students become familiar with the poem and its vocabulary. We have a discussion of the parts of the poem we like, and the things we think the writer has done well. These discussions affect the development of students' individual writing styles. We notice elements in the text that help us as readers. In "Boa Constrictor," for example, the repetitive nature of the language supports developing readers. We note how repeated words and phrases provide fast, easy clues for reading. We discuss the predictable pattern in the poem (as the constrictor progresses upward) and how it provides helpful cues in deciding what comes next. Students learn to attend to text structure as support for future reading. We also call to mind our personal experiences that relate to the poem, and brainstorm related writing ideas. With "Boa Constrictor," students may talk about being bitten by a pet or having a frightening experience with an animal. Students share their stories, and ideas for future writing are recorded on a list. Finally, we might engage in some dramatization of the poem.

Then we select the five Word Wall words. Again, these words need to have useful patterns. I invite my students to search for "words they like" or "colorful words" that do not have patterns already on the Word Wall. After sharing their ideas, we work together to test the utility of the pattern or patterns in each word. If *eaten* is chosen from "Boa Constrictor," for instance, we would first have to decide which rime in this two-syllable word to focus on: *eat* or *en*. Then we would try to think of many words with the same sound and spelling pattern. Let's look at the rime *eat*. *Eat* is an example of a pattern with variable spelling. Depending on the word, the sound made by *eat* may be spelled *eet*, as in *sheet*, or *eat*, as in *eaten*. Such patterns come up quite often and should not be cause for alarm. After all, this is the way it is in the English language. I simply share variations with students by

> *As you read the following sample dialogues, you'll notice I use the words "chunk" and "pattern" interchangeably with students. I do not consider the term "rime" to be user friendly for second graders, so I don't use it in my classroom. I hope the sample dialogues will give you a general feel for our classroom interaction.*

showing them examples of words with different spellings for the chunk and by explaining that they will see this rime spelled two ways. Chunks with the same spelling but different sounds also come up, though less frequently. If *dread* was chosen from "Boa Constrictor," we would think of words with the matching sound to test the utility of the rime *ead*. I'd show students how words like *bead* and *lead* have the same spelling pattern as *dread* but sound differently. These discussions build students' phonemic awareness, expose them to many patterns, and demonstrate their need to be flexible in their pattern use. Remember, rimes are much more reliable and helpful to students than letter-by-letter decoding instruction. Based on our success, I have confidence in the utility of the patterns, despite the fact that they may have more than one sound or variable spellings.

Our discussion about the possibility of *eat* as a pattern for the Wall might have proceeded in this way:

STUDENT: "I like the word *eaten.*"

TEACHER: "Great! There are two chunks in *eaten.* Remember a chunk or pattern is the vowel and what comes after it in each word part (syllable). Let's try the first chunk, *eat.* How many words can we come up with that have the chunk |*eat*|?"

STUDENTS AND TEACHER: *"Beat, neat, treat, meat, eat, wheat, feet, and sweet."*

TEACHER: "Now, that is a lot of words. I'd say the pattern *eat* could be helpful to us as readers and writers. So, *eaten* would be a good Word Wall word. What about the words *feet* and *sweet?* Let's try those on the board. Do they have the same spelling pattern as *eat* in *eaten?*" (Students help teacher to spell the words by calling out their spellings.) "Yes, those words say |*eet*| like *eat* in *eaten* but the sound that chunk makes can be spelled two ways. Both spellings are pretty common. You'll see those chunks in many words."

If we identify a student-chosen word as having a common pattern, as *eaten* was above, I write the word on a colorful card, which is cut to fit the outline of the word (see fig. 1). This makes it easier for students to visually distinguish between words (Cunningham, 1991). Also, I underline the pattern of interest. If we can derive only a few words from the pattern(s) in a selected word, we set it aside as uncommon, and do not add it to the Wall. I like to have one special Word Wall word for each highlighted pattern. So, with *eaten*, even though the rime in the second syllable of the word has the common pattern *en* (*En* can be determined to be common. It is found in: *ten, pen, wren, then, when, entangle,* etc.), a different word and card would be used to highlight that pattern.

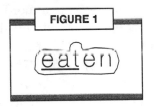

FIGURE 1

Referring again to "Boa Constrictor," let's test a few more words for usable patterns. If *constrictor* was offered by a student, and the rimes *on* and *or* were already on the Wall, would you conclude that *ict* is common? How many words can you think of with the *ict* pattern? I can add *strict*…but not too many other words come to mind. So, let's move on to another word in search of a pattern that is more common. What if a student chose *bit?* Test the pattern *it*. Many words come to mind: *fit, kitten, split, litter, sit,* and so on. This would be a good word for the Wall. Now, test other words from "Boa Constrictor" to determine which you might include for your reference wall.

Word Wall selection should take only a few minutes. Selection proceeds until we choose five words. We choose that number because my students seem to be comfortable learning five patterns within one week. You should feel free to propose words for the Wall, just as your students do. In this way, you can add specific patterns that student need to the Wall.

I like sharing power with my students: this involvement fosters a sense of ownership of the key words. Also, since the words are taken from favorite poems, there is an established memorable context for the Word Wall words.

You may be concerned about the commonality of the patterns in chosen words or with the order of pattern presentation. If so, you can again refer to the Benchmark lists or other word frequency lists like the Dolch Word Frequency List. The Dolch List contains the most routinely used words in our language. If the words found on this list have common patterns (some will be frequent words, but the rime will be uncommon), students may benefit by having these pat-

> *I have found that the poetry context provides another link that helps students to recall words and patterns. After all, we "play" with the new favorite intensively during the week and reread it throughout the year. This aids memory, recall, and familiarity with patterns.*

terns presented first because they will occur more regularly in what they read and write. Thus, students will quickly see the utility of the analogy lessons. For this reason, you may wish to begin the year by choosing Word Wall words yourself and then slowly increase student involvement in the process. Another helpful reference is the list of thirty-seven rimes previously mentioned. These are included in approximately five-hundred primary grade words compiled by Wylie and Durrell (1970). You can cross-reference these lists with the poetry used as you get your program going. However, this is an extra step that is not necessary for successful analogy instruction.

■　　■　　■　　■　　■

Favorites Folders. This activity relates to our method of Word Wall word selection. I developed the idea to help organize and store our new favorite poems. As mentioned, students receive a handwritten copy of the poems from which we extract our Word Wall words. They put their copies into their own manila folders labeled as the "Favorites Folder." For a few minutes each day, students work with a peer to read and enjoy the favorites of their choice from the folders. They are free to find a comfortable place in the room to work with their partners. Students read the poems by alternating voice patterns as we do in our whole class grouping. They also add dramatization and expression as desired. These repeated readings not only develop  students' awareness of Word Wall words and patterns, but promote fluency in reading and automaticity with sight vocabulary. Revisiting what they know is a positive step toward building confidence in reading ability. And my students love it! I hear them reciting poetry in the classroom, in the lunchroom, and on the playground!

■   ■   ■   ■   ■

Compiling the Word Wall. On Friday we add the five Word Wall words we practiced throughout the week to the Word Wall. The Word Wall becomes a permanent reference list that students may refer to as they read and write. It is useful for finding the sound of a rime to assist in decoding while reading. During writing, words on the Wall provide the possible spellings of various chunks. I make use of the wall daily in an integrated fashion. Its use is specifically highlighted in the reading strategy and challenge word minilessons.

We add words to the wall in alphabetical order, according to the first letter of the targeted rime. This letter will always be a vowel. The Wall is labeled with sections for *a, e, i, o* and *u* patterns to allow for easy reference. So, our Word Wall word *eaten* would be posed under the *e* patterns (see fig. 2). This is a better scheme for organization than putting the words on the Wall according to the first letters of the key words. I tried attaching words to the Wall in alphabetical order by initial letter and found the vowel scheme was more effective.

Why organize the Wall according to vowels? If spelling the word *carnivorous,* students might recall the spelling for the chunks in the first three syllables of the word. But they may need help for the final sound. They would listen for the sound of the chunk at the end of the word. Hearing the sound |*ous*|, they would then refer to the Wall for a possible spelling. If the Word Wall words are affixed to the wall according to their first letters, as with the *dread* example, students would be forced to recall the specific word that contains the pattern they are looking for. Our Word Wall word for *ous* was *fabulous* last year. Students would have to recall *fabulous* first, then look under the *f* section to find the *ous* spelling pattern. Sometimes recalling the Word Wall word can be accomplished with ease depending on how often the pattern is used. But the students have been exposed to so many patterns that recalling the specific key word for a pattern may prove difficult. If unable to recall a specific Word Wall word, students would then have to scan all of the patterns on the entire Wall to find the one they are looking for. This becomes a time-consuming process and thus defeats our purpose. If instead, the words are posted in the Wall according to the spelling of their rime, students hearing |ous| would possibly scan the *o* or *u* patterns for a match, while dismissing the *a, e* and *i* patterns as unlikely. This eliminates the need for students to first recall the key word when referring to a pattern. With *eat* from *eaten,* for example, students would immediately search under the *e* patterns because the beginning sound of the rime is obvious.

Arranging the Wall according to vowels also promotes ease of reference during reading. If readers come across the word *intimidate* and it is unfamiliar to them, they may readily decode *in* like *pin* and *tim* like *him* without even looking at the Wall. But what if they cannot recall the sound for *ate?* They may quickly refer to the Wall under the *a* patterns to find the Word Wall word that has the matching chunk, thereby revealing the sound for the rime and unlocking the mystery of the unknown word.

The following is an example of Word Wall organization according to the vowel scheme.

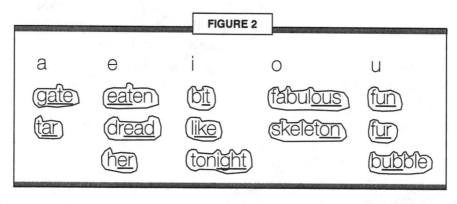

FIGURE 2

Glue Words. The Benchmark Program furnishes the teacher with a series of special words, referred to as "glue words," because they are connectors in sentences that "glue" other words together. These are common words that lack useful spelling patterns. Such patterns would not be practiced with students. Glue words are unrelated to the analogy strategies. They are examined here as an extension of the Word Wall.

Because glue words are in fact some of the most common in our language, they are put on the Wall so students can learn their spellings through continuous use. Knowledge of spelling patterns will not help students spell these words. Thus, it is a good idea to provide an easy reference so students can form the habit of spelling these common words correctly. If students continually misspell such words, they may develop automaticity for the incorrect spelling. Cunningham (1991) advocates having these words on the Wall, engaging in activities that promote their conventional spelling and automatic decoding, and emphasizing that they must be spelled correctly in writing. Instead of posting them on the Word Wall, I prefer to list these words on a separate wall because students will not be using their rimes to decode or inventively spell new words. We call this separate space our Help Wall. Students may also add these critical words to their spelling dictionaries. My own list of glue words was taken from a list of the 150 most frequent words in school English found in the American Heritage Word Frequency Book and summarized by Adams (1990, 274). They include:

a	of	they	which
again	one	through	who
any	only	to	with
are	people	two	you
because	said	use	your
been	some	very	
do	the	was	
	their	were	
have	there	what	
many	these	where	

Many more words appear on the frequency list. I have only included words with uncommon patterns here. You might refer to other lists to make appropriate additions.

We add glue words to our Help Wall as the need arises in our writing. I simply call students' attention to a word that is often misspelled. We may look at examples of how a common word has been misspelled and discuss the need for a conventional spelling. We "help" ourselves achieve this goal by adding that word to the Help Wall and referring to the Wall to develop the habit of spelling the word correctly. When students see a need for these words, as demonstrated in their own writing, they'll make real use of the Wall. I post glue words on the Wall alphabetically.

We use the Help Wall in other ways and add to it throughout the day when opportunities for learning come up during reading and writing. As the students demonstrate the need for a skill, like the need to know when to use *too, to,* or *two,* we look for examples in our reading and writing. When we find many samples, we examine them, discover a "rule" for their use, and add a reference to our Help Wall. In this example, cards with the words *too, to,* and *two* would be added to the Wall beside a small picture or sentence reminding students of their proper use.

We make many other useful references for readers and writers in our classroom, compiling lists of homonyms, compound words, synonyms, words we like, and so on. We create lists of words that follow peculiar rules, like words that drop the final *e* before an ending is added and words in which *y* is changed to *i* before a suffix. When we find examples of these words, we add them to our references. As students read and write, they may refer to the Help Wall and our class lists for aid in spelling or understanding a usage in text.

■   ■   ■   ■   ■

Shared Writing. After selecting the new Word Wall words, you may wish to create your own context from which words and patterns can be recalled. Students may write a story that incorporates the new Word Wall words and patterns. Reading the story fosters familiarity with patterns and fluency in reading. Students enjoy revisiting the story because they constructed it. I let the class know that when writers compose a story, they don't usually start with five words that they must include. Instead, they may start with a topic idea and some prewriting. This method may seem somewhat contrived, but I don't worry too much about that because we accomplish "real writing" throughout the year in Writing Workshop. Therefore, I know students understand the authentic process in addition to the "Word Wall" way of creating a story.

Our story often has elements similar to the new favorite poem. Together we produce the piece, recording topic ideas and phrases on chart paper first as a form of prewriting. We evaluate our choices and begin writing, revising, and changing ideas as we go. When we are satisfied with our draft, we rewrite the story on large chart paper. Students call out spellings and conventions so our final copy is correct, as a published piece should be. When we include a Word Wall word in the final copy of the story, we underline the pattern. Student volunteers illustrate the story, and we add it to the others on our poster chart. Then we use it as reading material in our Big Book, Poster, and Poetry Center.

■   ■   ■   ■   ■

Chant and Check. Once we've selected the Word Wall words and established a context, increased familiarity with the patterns must be built. One activity that does this is "chant and check" (Benchmark, 1986). Instead of just seeing and talking about chunks, students become fluent in their use through writing and interacting with the patterns. Again, student knowledge of patterns is critical in order to apply the analogy strategies efficiently.

We have written the five Word Wall words on cards. Every day of the school week we quickly practice the words. We accomplish this in a variety of ways. During chant and check, I hold up each word card, and ask students to give the word "a go." They attempt to write the word on scratch paper and underline the chunk without looking at the card. However, the card is available if needed. After I give students time to write, we chant and check. Students read the word, chant and point to it (tapping on the letters written on their paper), or clap the spelling. Then we recite the pattern. To further practice the rime and its use, we brainstorm other words with the same chunk and give those "a go." You could also use slates or dry erase boards for this activity.

At times, words offered do not follow the spelling pattern in the chosen Word Wall word. Again, this is a natural part of analogy instruction, and discussing each case familiarizes students with more patterns, sounds, and spellings.

For the Word Wall word *dread,* the activity might proceed as follows:

The teacher holds up the Word Wall word card.

Students read the card: *"Dread."*

TEACHER: "Yes, this is our Word Wall word *dread.* 'Oh dread, it's upmmmmmmmmmmmffffffff...' (extracting contextual phrase from the poem). What is the pattern in *dread?"*

STUDENTS: *"Ead."*

TEACHER: "Give *dread* a go on your scratch paper." (Students write the word and underline the pattern. The teacher allows appropriate wait time.) "Let's chant and check."

STUDENTS AND TEACHER *(chanting and pointing or clapping):* *"D-r-e-a-d* (spelling the word), *dread* (reading the word as a whole), *ead* (identifying the pattern as a whole), *e-a-d* (spelling the pattern)."

TEACHER: "Who can think of some other words with the pattern *ead* to try?" or "Who knows a word that rhymes?"

STUDENT: *"Bread."*

TEACHER: "Yes, give *bread* a go." After wait time, "Let's chant and check."

STUDENTS AND TEACHER: *"B-r-e-a-d."* (The teacher writes the spelling students offer for *bread* on the board while students chant and check their attempts on paper.) "Yes, *bread* has the *ead* pattern. It sounds and is spelled like our Word Wall word *dread.* If you know *dread,* you can spell and read *bread.* Let's try one more word with the *ead* chunk."

STUDENT: *"Fred."*

TEACHER:	"Okay. Give it a go" (After wait time) "Let's chant and check."
SOME STUDENTS:	*"F-r-e-d."*
OTHER STUDENTS:	*"F-r-e-a-d."*

The teacher writes the different spellings that are heard for Fred *on the chalkboard.*

TEACHER:	"I hear some different spellings. This is what I heard." (The teacher points to the different spellings and reviews each with students). "Which one looks correct to you? Which have you seen before?"

With students' assistance, it is concluded that "F-r-e-d" *is the common spelling.*

TEACHER:	"Notice how the chunk *ed* in *Fred* does sound like the *ead* chunk in *dread.* Here's another example of a different spelling for the same chunk. *Ed* is a common chunk, too. You'll see it in more words."

You may add an additional level to this activity. Have students insert or delete a letter to change a word and/or its pattern. For example, after correctly spelling *Fred,* you may say, "Now add the letter *i* to make a new word and pattern." Chant and check for the spelling of *fried.* At that point, you may even try to come up with a few analogous words for the newly created pattern to have "a go" with. From such an activity, students gain an understanding that changing just one letter transforms the whole word. The idea was adapted from Cunningham's "Making Words" lessons (1992).

Procedures for the chant and check activity may be varied. For instance, students may select the next word to be practiced by having to sort through the five new words of the week for a pattern match. Teachers might say, "If I was writing a letter to *Nate,* which Word Wall word could I use to help me spell his name?" Students then identify the Word Wall word with the analogous pattern (i.e., *gate*) and the chant and check activity proceeds.

A more challenging variation is to have students give the Word Wall word 'a go' after being shown a card and write a few of their own analogous words before the word is read, spelled, and worked on with the class. Teachers may say, "Give this word 'a go' (holding up a Word Wall card) and try some words you can think of with the same pattern." In this way, students are required to independently read the word card and search their own memory stores for pattern matches. This assures that all students are engaging in activity that promotes the sorting and matching abilities necessary to apply analogy in reading and writing. The class next chants and checks the Word Wall word. Volunteers supply analogous words and spellings that are recorded on the board and discussed.

In her book, Cunningham (1991) offers a multitude of different activities for working with patterns. I have adapted her examples to make variations on the basic Benchmark ideas. She suggests that a variety of activities using different methods may more effectively reach all learners. Activities like "Making Words" with letter-card manipulatives, matching and sorting words according to patterns, and using books to "round up" words with patterns to add to class charts all may be utilized for pattern investigation and review.

The chant and check activities should last only a few minutes, keeping review time minimal. Just seconds are spent on each Word Wall word or brainstormed word. This fast pace holds students' attention and exposes them to many words and patterns. Additionally, students have multisensory experiences when engaged in the above activities. They see, write, chant, and clap or point to words. Varying needs and abilities are addressed as students call out or I offer a range of analogous words to have "a go" with. Simple one-syllable words should be worked with (as in the dialogue example), in addition to more difficult multisyllabic words.

Practice Pages and Practice Folders. This is another activity I developed to assist students in gaining automatic recognition of patterns. I felt my students could use supplementary practice and exposure to spelling patterns in addition to the chant and check activity advocated in The Benchmark Program. I wanted practice and exposure to patterns formerly presented to continue throughout the year. Remember, automaticity in decoding is a skill good readers have and poor readers lack. Again, automaticity is the key to freeing up the mental capacities of students so that attention is focused on meaning-making in text. The importance of automaticity drove me to include the practice pages and folders in our day-to-day activities.

The practice pages are very similar to the chant and check activity except that a permanent copy of the Word Wall words, extracted patterns, and related brainstormed words is created. This activity, then, is not done on scratch paper. Halfway through each week, I prepare a work space that contains the new Word Wall words and their highlighted patterns. This usually occurs on Wednesday, after students have already had some practice with the patterns. I include a context-rich sentence containing each Word Wall word. Students and teacher can work together to develop these sentences, but in the interest of time I create the sentence before presenting the practice pages to students. The practice page is duplicated, and each student is given a copy to fill in. We work together cooperatively as we follow the chant and check procedure. The first Word Wall word is read and the pattern repeated orally. I then ask, "Who can think of a word that has the same pattern or chunk as the Word Wall word?" Students volunteer words, and we use the pattern in the Word Wall word to spell the new word. Students cross-check their answers as they assist me in finding the correct spelling. The correct spelling is recorded on the chalkboard, and students record it under the matching pattern on the practice page. Two or three words with matching patterns are also recorded on the page.

For example, with the Word Wall word *eaten, eaten* is read as a whole, the target chunk is read (*eat*), and alternative words with matching patterns are offered. Words like *beat, meatloaf,* and *wheat* would be recorded on the practice page because the spelling of the rime matches the Word Wall word. As expected, words without matching spellings for the sound of the pattern are sometimes volunteered. These are dealt with as before. They are written on the board and discussed. The students are reminded that chunks that sound identical sometimes have different spelling patterns. Words with the same sounding rimes but different spellings are not recorded on the practice page. So, if our Word Wall word is *eaten, sweeter* would not be recorded under the rime *eat*. If the alternative spelling for the rime is common, as chunks with different spelling patterns often are, the alternative pattern will surely be practiced at another time during the year. Teachers depending on their own resources for Word Wall word choices could stop and quickly record the pattern for future instruction.

When the practice page is completed, we fold the side with Word Wall and analogous words under, hiding the sentences. The folded strip provides a quick review list, but the sentences remain available to assist students in decoding an unknown word. Using lists with available contexts to develop fluency is an idea I garnered from Don Holdaway (1980), a teacher-educator from Australia. I remind students that if they come to a word they don't know, they may refer to the sentences to figure out the word from the meaning of the whole sentence. This strategy reinforces the use of context to determine meaning while reading. I have not often observed students using the aid of the contexts in the sentences on the practice pages. This is because they are already quite familiar with the Word Wall words based on their involvement in word selection, creating a language experience story, chant and check, and repeated rereadings of the new favorite. However, this is an option that is always accessible to students, just as contexts are always available during the authentic act of reading connected text. I strive to make all activities as real-life as possible.

Once the paper folding is done, students buddy up with a partner. They practice the patterns of the week through peer tutoring. My students love to engage in student/teacher role plays. The "teacher" points to the Word Wall words, the patterns, and the corresponding words, moving down the list as the student reads. As one practice page is finished, peer teachers praise students, and a previously completed practice page is read. If students make mistakes during their review, "teachers" ask them to try again and prompt them to use the sentence if needed. The sentence includes the Word Wall word that is the key to the sound of the pattern in the unknown word. Students reverse roles as desired, always allowing each to have a chance as teacher and student. Practice pages are stored in manila folders. We call these our "Practice Folders." Each student has a folder so labeled to distinguish it from our "Favorites Folder."

We make one more addition to our Practice Folders. As mentioned with "glue words," there are some simple sight words in our language that lack frequent patterns. Many of these are extremely common, and most learners develop fluency with them through their reading and writing experiences. Choral, cooperative, and repeated readings, in addition to modeled and process writing, are especially helpful for developing sight-word proficiency. Since knowledge of patterns is not as useful with these words, we add a few lists of them to our Practice Folders to ensure that all students develop automaticity with these essential connecting elements. On these pages, words are listed to the left and corresponding context sentences at the right. These are folded and utilized like the practice pages with Word Wall patterns. Teachers may refer to word frequency references to create lists of useful connecting words that lack common patterns.

The Practice Folder is used on a daily basis. My students love working with buddies in the folder because of the quick interaction involved. The peer tutoring sessions last no more than three to four minutes. Many previous patterns are reviewed as the folders are compiled throughout the year.

Some might call the practice pages and Practice Folder contrived activities unrelated to real reading and writing. I strive to make the activities as authentic as possible while bolstering my students' automaticity with the patterns they will encounter as readers and writers. The practice pages are an efficient way for students to achieve this. Such mastery of patterns seems to promote significant progress as you'll note when you examine samples of my students' work. Control at these basic levels may promote achievement at higher levels. Of course, any activity must be evaluated for its real utility and benefit to specific students before it is added to the classroom curriculum. Based on my own analysis, I will continue to include the practice pages and folders in our day because these few minutes contribute to a lifetime of easy access to the code of our language.

Reading Strategy Lessons. Another minilesson adapted from The Benchmark Program, this daily activity reinforces how the decoding by analogy strategy can be applied in connected text. This, of course, is a goal different from the development of automaticity with patterns. I prepare two sentences on sentence strips with one challenging word in each. The challenge word is underlined, and the sentences are examined one at a time with students.

During the reading strategy lessons, I emphasize the integrated use of all cues available to the reader to make meaning from the sentence. When I present the reading strategy lessons, I tell students to say "blank" for the underlined word as we read the sentence the first time. I emphasize that the unknown, or challenge, word might be discovered through context. If students come up with meaningful hypotheses for the word at this point, we check their predictions against the sounds in the word.

If students cannot decode the word through use of context alone, we then reread the sentence, noting the beginning sound of the challenge word. That clue, coupled with the context of the sentence, may yield the unknown word. The students are also aware that they may skip the unknown word if the meaning of the sentence is not affected. I always emphasize that reading is, first and foremost, making meaning. Getting at the story is our main goal. But if these strategies fail, we go back to the unknown word and look for the chunks. We compare the rimes in the challenge word to the patterns on the Word Wall and other words from memory. This comparison enables students to discover the pronunciation of the challenge word through recognition of similar chunk sounds.

Often, students don't have to decode in order for the challenge word to be revealed. Instead, when they decode a few parts of the word, and these sounds are coupled with the meaning of the sentence, the challenge word is disclosed. We always go back and reread the sentence to make sure the discovered challenge word makes sense.

During the second half of the year, unknown words become increasingly more difficult. I want to continue challenging students to develop their strategies. If the word, once decoded, is still beyond the students' vocabularies, we use the meaning of the sentence to uncover the meaning of the word. Hence, students broaden their vocabularies and they practice a strategy to help them understand advanced words in more difficult text.

In developing sentence strips for reading strategy lessons, I try to vary the types of challenge words used and the kinds of cues available in the sentences. After all, I would not always want the challenge word to be discovered by context alone. I would also be foolish to use words that students could always skip without affecting the meaning of the sentence. If these were the circumstances, students would never experience the usefulness of the decoding-by-analogy strategy or practice other helpful cues. I construct sentences relative to the students' experiences so they will be meaningful. Because students know that the reading strategy sentences contain meaningful messages, they are interested.

The challenging word is one my students will probably be unfamiliar with, and it may or may not contain patterns that are on the Word Wall. This is the way it is in real reading. Not all chunks of words unknown by students in text will be on the Wall. Therefore, I encourage them to use their memory store and other sources of words around the classroom, like word lists or posters, to decode by analogy. This promotes flexible use of the strategy.

With my group of students, the challenge words are always multisyllabic so that they are less likely to recognized by sight. This also encourages attention to the chunks in the word. Of course, at the beginning of the school year, the words are more simple and carefully chosen in order to demonstrate the ease and utility of the strategy to students. For example, I will be certain, when first introducing students to the reading strategy lessons, that the challenge words included in the sentences contain rimes already on the wall. You will need to adjust the types of challenge words used in your lessons to suit the needs of your students in order to assure success.

I have found a thesaurus to be an excellent resource for challenge words. Multisyllabic synonyms for familiar words make good challenge words.

■ Sample Reading Strategy Lesson

Now, let's try a hypothetical example of a reading strategy lesson based on what typically happens in my classroom. I might construct a reading strategy sentence centered around a book we are reading, like *The Three Robbers* by Tomi Ungerer. Here's the sentence:

In *The Three Robbers,* the robbers are <u>*merciless*</u> to their victims.

We start by reading the entire sentence, saying <u>blank</u> for the underlined word. (My students would understand from experience that the book title needs to be underlined and is not the challenge word.)

TEACHER:	"Given the meaning of the sentence, what might the unknown word be?" (I often cover the word with my hand at this point to encourage students to use the context alone to make predictions.)
STUDENTS:	*"Wicked, cruel."*
TEACHER:	"Those words do make sense in the sentence, and as readers, if we were stuck, we could substitute one of these words to make meaning from the sentence. Then we could go on reading our story without further interruption. Substituting a word that makes sense for an unknown word is a good strategy, but it does not always work. So, let's try something else."
TEACHER:	(Uncovering the challenge word) "Do either of those words (*cruel* or *wicked*) match the sounds we see in the unknown word?"
STUDENTS:	"No." (Since the sounds in *cruel* and *wicked* do not, we move to looking at the beginning sound of the unknown word.)
TEACHER:	"What is the first sound in the unknown word?"
STUDENTS:	*"|m|."*
TEACHER:	"If the beginning sound in the challenge word is |m|, what word or words can you think of that make sense in the sentence and begin with that sound?"
STUDENT:	*"Mean."*

TEACHER:	"Yes, *mean* starts with |m| and makes sense, but does this word (pointing to the unknown word) look like *mean?* What else can we do as readers to figure out the unknown word?"
STUDENTS:	"Look at the chunks."
TEACHER:	"What chunks do you see that you know or that you can find on the Word Wall or elsewhere?"

Students and I work together to apply the decoding-by-analogy strategy.

STUDENTS AND TEACHER:	"I see the chunk *er* like in the Word Wall word *her,* so that must be *mer.*" (The middle rime might be skipped as not having a familiar pattern [if seen as *ci*], or it may be decoded based on its similarity to the rime *ill* as in our Word Wall word *will,* depending on how the students divide the word. Keep in mind that not all chunks must be decoded. A sampling of the sounds, coupled with the context, will undoubtedly reveal the word.) "The last chunk is *ess* like in the word *dress* so that must say *less.* The word is *merciless.*"

Once the word is decoded, we would discuss how *merciless* does mean about the same as *mean, wicked,* or *cruel.* We might then add the colorful new word to our dictionaries in the thesaurus section under synonyms for *mean.* My students are always on the lookout for colorful synonyms for commonly used words that we may use as writers.

After working with students on another reading strategy sentence, I always ask, "Now what did we do as readers to figure out these challenging words?" Together, we review the strategies we used and how they were helpful to us in constructing meaning, which again, is what reading is.

We do not follow a set sequence of strategies when attacking an unknown word, as it may appear from the discussion above. At times I lead students, but I often let *them* lead the process. I do not want to have to prompt them to use strategies. Instead, I want them to become adept at knowing how and when to use their reading strategies independently.

As we get our momentum going throughout the year, students mostly lead the reading strategy lessons. We discuss the strategies they propose us to use. I have observed that students rely heavily on the decoding-by-analogy strategy to deal with reading problems. It often seems to be the first strategy they use, in combination with context, when they come upon an unknown word in text. This could be because they understand the strategy well, realize its utility, can apply it easily, and find it quicker to use than the alternative strategies.

Cunningham (1991) offers variations on employing the reading strategy lesson. Sentences may be written on an overhead projector with the challenge word covered for the students to predict. As predictions are checked, the word is slowly revealed. Alternatively, sentence strips may be used with the challenge word folded under at the end. When the strip is turned over, the challenge word alone is shown first and students are asked to write words they know that are analogous to as many chunks as they can (if the word is polysyllabic). Then they use their words to decode the chunks in the challenge word. Or, on an easier level, they are asked to match the challenge word with a rhyming word from a few key word choices. Teachers may say, "Write the word that rhymes (from the choices) with the challenge word," or "Write the word that will help us read the challenge word." After recording a match independently, the students use it to decode the challenge word saying, for example, "If my word is *right,* then the challenge word must be *flight.*" The sentence is then revealed, and they check their prediction for meaning. Every pupil is encouraged to respond. Independence in sorting and matching is promoted when students are asked to write analogous words for the challenge word before working on decoding by analogy as a class. Additionally, through writing, the activity becomes kinesthetic rather than just visual and auditory.

We always follow the reading strategy lessons with reading of real, connected text. This is usually done through whole-class shared reading of a big book and then followed by guided reading sessions for smaller groups. I feel it is very important to go directly from the lessons to a more authentic type of reading, where students can now apply, and I can model, the strategies we have just practiced. When we come across an unfamiliar word in the book we are reading, we utilize the same strategies applied in our lessons. At first, I talk aloud about how to use strategies in text, exposing the students to what I would do as a reader. Using this method, I provide them with a model to follow within whole texts. I also use Post-its to mask challenging words in the book and allow the students to talk through the strategies for decoding the word. Of course, natural occurrences of challenging words are frequent and do not have to be planned. Through the reading strategy lessons and real reading of an assortment of texts, students experience the strategies in varied settings and can transfer their learning to useful contexts.

■　　■　　■　　■　　■

Challenge Words. As the school year was underway, the reading strategy lessons were working well for fostering use of decoding by analogy in reading. But I wanted a minilesson for directly teaching the analogy strategy for use in writing. This is what I designed the challenge word activity to do. Of course, I also model the strategy in authentic writing contexts during composition.

One or two days a week, just before writing workshop, I call students to the rug with their writing workshop folders and a piece of scratch paper. I ask them to offer words that we can attempt to spell inventively using the strategies we know. I make sure the words we try range from easier, one-syllable words to more difficult polysyllabic words so all students are successful. This is especially important at the beginning of the year when students are just starting to develop the analogy strategies. We use the patterns on the Word Wall and others from memory to practice quickly coming up with possible spellings. Students can offer any real word for a challenge word. Therefore, not all patterns contained in the challenge words are on the

Wall. Students must rely on all available resources, including their own memory of patterns they have seen, to apply the analogy strategy for inventing spellings. As discussed, students also typically do this during reading strategy lessons. (Note that we have discussed two types of challenge words: one for reading and now one for writing.)

For instance, a student may challenge us to try the word *investigate*. Students give it "a go," listening for the chunks they hear in the word and using other words they know to come up with a spelling on their scratch papers. All students can be successful (even with a more difficult challenge word like this) at writing a probable spelling for at least some of the chunks. After time for thinking, student volunteers share their invented spellings and I write their attempts on the board or overhead projector. We compare their attempts to patterns we know and to words we have seen in our own experience as readers and writers. If two or three spellings seem probable and have logical patterns that work with the sounds we hear in the challenge word, I ask students, "Which spelling do you think is best? Which have you seen in your reading or in other places?" or simply, "Which one looks right to you?" Students are often able to distinguish the correct spelling by sight. If not, sometimes we will consult a dictionary or, in the interest of time, I will provide the correct spelling. Students are then invited to add the word to their spelling dictionaries if they like the word and feel they may use it as writers.

With the word *investigate,* students could reasonably offer: *envestigat, invistigate,* and *investigate.* Once these are written for all to examine, we evaluate each attempt.

TEACHER: (pointing to the first attempt) "Let's look at our first try. What a good start! *En* could be the spelling of the first chunk because it sounds like our Word Wall word *pen.* Look at the next chunk. *Vest* works, too. It sounds like our Word Wall word *best.* Then I hear |i| like *igloo* or |ig| like our Word Wall word *pig.* Now how about that last chunk? *A-t. A-t* sounds like the word *hat* to me. What is the last chunk you hear in *investigate?*

STUDENTS: "|*ate*|."

TEACHER:	"Do you think *a-t* is probably the spelling for that last chunk then?" (I work with students to help them understand that the sound in hat is different from the sound in the last syllable of the challenge word [gate]. We would rule out this spelling and attempt to correct the error.)
TEACHER:	"What is a word you know that has the chunk |ate|?"
STUDENTS:	(using the Wall, their memories, or other sources to find a better match) *"Hate, date, late, wait."*
TEACHER:	"Good! All of those words say |ate|. How is the *ate* chunk spelled in those words?"
STUDENTS:	*"A-t-e."*
TEACHER:	"How is |ate| spelled in *wait?"* (With student help, *wait* is written correctly on the board.) "Since we came up with two spellings for the *ate* chunk, either may be correct. Let's try both endings." (Both are written at the end of the spelling attempt). "Which looks best?"
STUDENTS:	*"A-t-e."*
TEACHER:	"That could be the spelling for the last chunk we hear in *investigate."*

Envestigate is a more logical spelling than *envestigat.* We then move on and evaluate the other spelling attempts. I often ask students to explain their procedure in developing a spelling. They describe their strategies, like how they used the Word Wall, their memory, or another reference to find the spelling of a chunk. After analyzing and working with a few of the possible spelling variations, we visually analyze each choice to determine the correct spelling (as in the chant and check activity). The practice and analysis that the Challenge Word activity supplies build phonemic awareness and demonstrate what real writers do in determining a spelling.

After assessing our invented spellings for *investigate*, students may think twice about using *at* to spell the *ate* chunk. Or the lesson may help them in other, untold ways to better self-evaluate what they do as they spell inventively. Such discussion enhances their knowledge of letter-sound relationships and pushes them toward continuous growth and refinement in their strategy use.

Again, if students offer a challenge word that contains chunks not on the wall, I encourage them to think of other words they know with the same sound. In the *investigate* example, any one of those rimes might not have been on the wall, but simple words with the same rimes could easily be thought of and used to spell by analogy. The Word Wall does not have to be fully filled to use the analogy strategies in reading and writing. Students are encouraged to use their knowledge beyond the limitations of the Wall. Any word that is analogous to a word being read or written, wherever it may come from, is useful.

Of course, many challenge words will not be spelled conventionally. Our goal here is to provide students with quick, independent strategies for inventing spellings. As previously mentioned, the invented spellings students produce using the analogy strategy are much closer to the correct spelling of words than attempts made by relying on individual letter-sounds. The author's intended message comes through clearly, based on the sounds of the chunks. If the word is spelled as it sounds, the students will have a likely spelling. My students sometimes choose to use dictionaries and other references when editing their writing. Correct spellings are often more easily found based on attempts constructed by analogy. Students using analogy can develop likely variations of how a word may be spelled to cross-check with a dictionary. Remember the reference to the old strategy of spelling a word as it sounds by stretching it like a rubber band to hear every sound? Not only do students struggle to hear isolated sounds, but because the individual letter-sound correspondences are so unreliable, the invented spelling that results is often indiscernible.

So, during the challenge word activity, if we work to spell a word by analogy that is not true to its sound, I simply praise logical results. An example would be if a student inventively spells the word *viewed: v e w e d* using the rime in the word *few*. We evaluate how the invented spelling clearly provides the sounds of the word and communicates well what the author means in a rough draft. I follow up with a comment like, "Yes, that's a good possible spelling. But this is another one of those words you have to know by heart in order to spell correctly. Of course, if you were really concerned you could look in a dictionary or ask an expert. But, in your rough draft, getting your ideas down before they're forgotten is what matters. You can always go back and fix spelling mistakes. Spell words quickly in a way that makes sense, and move forward with your writing!" If the word is commonly used, I remind students they should refer to the glue words to develop the habit of spelling it correctly. Or we make an addition to the Help Wall if the word fits the characteristics of a glue word.

When we finish inventively spelling and discussing a few challenge words, I review with students why we engaged in the activity. We acknowledge that these are the strategies we can directly apply as we compose rough drafts during Writing Workshop. We like to think of it as an occasional warm-up for writing. Authentic writing always follows the short challenge word activity. I may follow up with modeled writing, wherein I show students how I use the strategy during the real act of composing a whole text. As students go forth to work on their own writing, they have the opportunity to immediately apply the strategy they have practiced and seen modeled.

The invented spelling activity may be adapted to a much easier level by providing students with only a few key word choices from which to spell new words by analogy (Cunningham, 1991). Students who are at the early stages of developing the ability to look and sort for patterns may need fewer possibilities to search than the entire Word Wall or one's memory store. For example, students may be provided with the Word Wall words *joy, bone, house,* and *coat.*

A criticism of invented spelling is that students might form bad habits by practicing incorrect spellings. This can indeed occur with common words that are continuously practiced incorrectly (as discussed in our glue word section). However, this is not true for less common words that are written and invented infrequently because students do not tend to form repeated habits with these words (Cunningham, 1991).

The teacher may ask, "Which word can I use to help me write my story about a *mouse?*" Students then draw an analogy from the word *house* to spell *mouse* on their papers. The probable spelling for *mouse* might even be discussed first, before students write, to ensure success for all learners. Rather, invented spelling is one way for emerging writers to communicate and serves as a developmental step toward conventional spelling. Research has shown that students who read and write prolifically and attend to spelling patterns move through stages toward conventional spelling (Henderson, 1990). Additionally, invented spelling has been shown to help students become better decoders as they apply and refine their letter-sound knowledge (Clarke, 1988). Analogy provides students with a method for spelling very advanced words which, as second graders for example, they would not be expected to know how to spell conventionally. When you examine the writing samples, you will see how students move toward a higher percentage of conventional spellings as they compose throughout the year.

Clarke, L.K. (1988). Invented versus traditional spelling in first graders' writings: Effects on learning to spell and read. *Research in the Teaching of English, 22,* 281-309.

Cunningham, P.M. (1991). *Phonics they use: Words for reading and writing.* New York: HarperCollins.

Cunningham, P.M. (1992). Making words: Enhancing the invented spelling-decoding connection. *The Reading Teacher, 46, 106-115.*

Henderson, E. (1990). *Teaching spelling.* Boston, MA: Houghton Mifflin.

Holdaway, D. (1980). *Independence in reading.* Portsmouth, NH: Heinemann.

Integrating Analogy
Instruction into a Holistic
Reading/Writing Daily Program

■ Sample Schedule

Following is a sample schedule demonstrating how the Analogy
Minilessons are included in a typical day of instruction. Notice the
quick pace of the activities and how they are carefully sequenced to
provide varying experiences for students. Activities of the same type
are not scheduled back-to-back. Careful sequencing keeps students
motivated. Also, minilessons and practice sessions are always followed by authentic reading and writing activities. Based on this
schedule, students have opportunities to apply directly what they are

learning. Times listed in the schedule are approximate and vary daily depending on student need and interest.

I must emphasize that this is only a sample of what a daily schedule may look like. It worked well last year for my students and me. Next year, it may change. I hope you will change it to fit your needs and beliefs about what makes good practice.

APPROXIMATE TIME	POSSIBLE ACTIVITY
9:00-9:15:	Optional Journal Writing
	Book Box Book and Reading Log and/or silent reading of self-selected books, possibly combined with writing in Reading Log
	Buddy sharing and class sharing of journals
9:15-9:30:	Book Share with buddies and class sharing
9:30-9:40:	Modeled writing: Daily News
9:40-9:50:	Read aloud
9:50-10:00:	New Favorite Poem activities (introduction, repeated readings, and dramatization)
10:00-10:10:	Word Wall activities:
	Monday: Word Wall selection possibly followed by Shared Writing (10:10-10:20)
	Wednesday: Complete new Practice Page for Word Wall words of the week
	Tuesday, Thursday, and Friday: Alternative Pattern Investigation or Help Wall activities
10:10-10:15:	Practice Folders: review previous practice pages with buddy
10:15-10:20:	Favorites Folders: reread old favorites with a buddy
10:20-10:25:	Morning Message
10:25-10:40:	Reading and Writing Centers: Big Book, Poster and Poetry Message Center Listening Center

Library Contor: Hotorogoneous guided reading group

RECESS BREAK

Time	Activity
10:55-11:05:	Chant and Check variations or Alternative Pattern Review activity
11:05-11:10:	Reading Strategy lesson
11:10-11:25:	Shared reading with a big book and/or class novel
11:25-11:40:	Reading Workshop Individual, buddy, group reading and logs + reading centers Homogeneous guided reading groups
11:40-11:45:	Challenge words
11:45-11:55:	Writing workshop minilesson and topic list review
11:55-12:00:	Silent writing time
12:00-12:20:	Open workshop time and student/teacher conferences
12:20-12:30:	Writing workshop class sharing time

LUNCH BREAK

Time	Activity
1:05-1:25:	SQUIRT: "sustained, quiet, uninterrupted, individual reading time"

We've all heard the saying "Make every minute count." I strive to do exactly that with our class time. However, it takes a while to become familiar with the teaching approach. Allow yourself time to become accustomed to the instruction, just as you allow students time to develop and make mistakes as learners. Once you and your students become comfortable, things move along more quickly and, if you wish, everything in the schedule above can be fit into your day. Believe it or not, extra time between lessons and workshops even becomes available. I usually capitalize on this time by sharing a few new books through book talks and reading aloud to my students.

Many examples and practical ideas exist for making the mini-lessons and analogy strategies fit into authentic reading and writing. I have purposely highlighted analogy strategies more than others to emphasize how I use the particular strategies of interest in this book. In addition, I have included detailed descriptions of the reading and writing activities themselves. These are designed to help teachers who are making broad changes in their basic approaches to literacy instruction.

■   ■   ■   ■   ■

Journals. We often start our day with journal writing. When students first enter the classroom, they have the option of writing in their journals. I make it clear that they do not need to write in their journals every day. Instead, they write when they feel they have something of importance to record. We have our own books in which to keep thoughts on daily happenings, ideas for future writing, and drawings or notes. I quickly take care of school business, such as attendance, and then, if I have something important to record, I write in my journal.

Journal writing becomes the first opportunity of the day to model using the analogy strategy and other strategies, too. As I write in my journal, I think aloud. I disclose to students what I am thinking as I write and how I am solving writing problems, including how I use the analogy strategy and the Word Wall to spell.

For example, if I were to write the message: "My cat fell out a twenty-foot high window," I might think aloud saying, "Let's see. I'd like to write down what happened to my cat last night. *My,* I'm starting a sentence so I need a capital. I know how to spell *my.* That's easy to remember: *m-y. Cat, cat* is another easy word that I automatically know how to spell. *Fell, fell* sounds like the Word Wall word *smell.* The sound I hear at the beginning of *fell* is |f| so I need the letter *f.* Now, I'll add the chunk from *smell. Fell* is *f-e-l-l. Out* is like *shout* and *a* is easy. *Twenty* is more difficult. As I listen for the chunks, I hear |twen| and then |ty|. I know a word that sounds the same as |twen|, it is *when.* If *when* is spelled *w-h-e-n,* then |twen| must be *t-w-e-n.* The second part I hear |ty| sounds like the second part in *bony.* I bet |ty| is spelled *t-y.*"

Another relevant point can be mentioned here. When my students use the analogy strategy to spell, I am not too concerned about where they break the word into syllables to encode the onset and rime. I simply emphasize that we should listen for the chunks, but as with the word *twenty,* students may hear the breaks in the word differently from what is absolutely correct. Perhaps a student would hear *twent* and *y* as parts. The analogy strategy would still be successful, as a student likens |*twent*| to the Word Wall word *tent* and *y* to the word bony.

During journal time, in addition to whole-class modeling, I may walk around the room writing a line or two in response to what students are writing in their journals. I can quickly think aloud at students' desks as I respond to their writing. Writers are also free to come to the rug and wait for someone who would like to share. They may dialogue back and forth about what has been written in their journals. I also call everyone together for some class sharing time. Volunteers read from their journals, and we listen for stories, recording topic ideas on our Writing Workshop topic list when appropriate.

■　　■　　■　　■　　■

Book Box. If students choose not to write in their journals, they have the option of selecting a book to read from our class library or working with a Book Box book. I put together boxes of books that are organized according to reading level. Once a week, students go to their book box and select a book to read and respond to in their reading logs. The reading log is a dialogue journal in which students communicate with peers and with me about books. While I value free, unconstrained selection of books for reading, I began using the book boxes last year in an effort to gear one choice per week to assured success. I have found that the book boxes allow students freedom of choice within a particular range. Of course, they can respond to any book at any time in

their log as well. I find the marriage between self-selection and guided selection to be a necessary yet happy one.

I keep a reading log, which I often share with students. As with journal writing, at times I think aloud in the presence of students as I write in my log. I model the analogy strategy for writing and the proper use of conventions. I talk about the type of information I am recording in the log based on my reading. At times I respond to a student's log in front of the class (with the student's permission), thinking aloud about appropriate responses as well as my strategy use. In this way, I provide students with a model of what a responder might do. They imitate that model as they dialogue with each other in journals and logs. Students are welcome to share with each other, and they turn in their logs for my response as they complete entries during the week.

■　　　■　　　■　　　■　　　■

Book Share. We follow up journal writing and book box with book talks. Each evening, students read at home to or with family members. Their progress is recorded on a home-school correspondence record. Students may check out books for home reading from our class library, peers, the school library, or the local library. Naturally, books from home are also welcomed reading material. The books read at home are brought to school each morning. I call students together to find a buddy and share their books. They tell what their books are about, what they liked, share a favorite picture, and so on. The idea is to spread enthusiasm for new titles.

We have a class sharing time. Two or three titles are shared by students, and I always share a few from around the room. On occasion, to emphasize use of decoding by analogy, we look for patterns in book titles being shared and discuss how the chunks are helpful to readers. Also, students may report how they solved a reading problem by using the analogy strategy or other strategies during reading.

Book Share promotes reading at home, allows students to verbalize about their reading, exposes them to many titles, and generally gets them involved in the literate community of our classroom.

Daily News. I select one student to share a statement about an event in his/her life or anything else he/she wishes to share with the group. We talk about the statement, perhaps even adding a writing idea to our Writing Workshop topic list. Next I repeat the news statement, making sure I have the student's words. Then I record the News in front of the class on large chart paper.

I vary my approach to recording the News. Some days, I think aloud about the student's statement as I write it, modeling the analogy strategy for spelling combined with the use of writing conventions to accurately record the News. This think-aloud sounds much the same as the example you read in the journal activity description. On other days, I put my marker on the chart paper, repeating the sound or the word I am about to record, while the students call out what I should do.

For example, if a student's news was, "My bedroom in the basement flooded last night," I would start by saying, "My, my, I hear |m|… Students would then call out, "M, you need an m." Or, "Capital M. It's starting a sentence." I then hold up my hand to signal them to stop, and we talk about which option would be correct. When we decide, we move on. Students shout out possible spellings using analogies. Sometimes they offer multiple spellings, and I may quickly pass out dictionaries to groups. They work cooperatively to search for the correct spelling from the student-generated options on the board. To help them understand dictionary use, I also think aloud and model how I found a word or possible spelling using a dictionary. Another option for dealing with spelling choices is to list the possibilities and visually discriminate to decide the correct spelling. This was also modeled in the Challenge Word activity.

I prefer to write the News on chart paper so it becomes a permanent record placed in our Message Center for future rereadings. Some teachers enjoy binding the chart paper News from each month into a big book, which is added to the classroom library. A variation of this is to record the News on an overhead while thinking aloud or allowing the students to assist. Teachers of upper grades may like the News to be a summary of the day or period, having one student record the News in a log as a reference for absent students. This may also be considered a written record of class history.

■   ■   ■   ■   ■

Read Aloud. Through Read Alouds students experience the delight of enjoying another good book. They are also exposed to different writing styles. They can learn about genres and the craft of writing. Reading aloud can also promote topic generation for students' own process writing.

While reading aloud, I sometimes model how I solve reading problems. If the print is large, I can show students where I am in a text and share aloud my thinking on how to decode a word using context and analogy. I may also skip or substitute a word, all in the pursuit of understanding the meaning of the story.

For example, last year I shared Graeme Base's version of Jabberwocky with students. This book has many nonsense terms and can give an adult a good lesson in the utility of the decoding-by-analogy strategy. Before reading the book aloud, the students and I previewed the pictures and sampled the text, trying to get a sense of what the book was about. While we made these predictions, I pointed to the title and said, "This is a strange word. But I think I can read it. I see *jab* like *dab, ber* like *her, wock* like *lock* and *y* like *bony.* The title is Jabberwocky! Now I wonder what a Jabberwocky is?..." Our discussion continued from there, but I was able to get in just a short bit of modeling, showing how and when to use decoding by analogy, even in the authentic context of reading aloud to students.

■   ■   ■   ■   ■

New Favorite Poem Activities. Here are a few additional

ideas for using poetry. First, during a rereading of the new poem, have students look for patterns different from the Word Wall words of the week. They may also brainstorm related words that contain these new patterns. You can ask if students made use of patterns to decode any unknown words and discuss their examples.

The new favorite poem is a great source for teaching about conventions and stylistic elements in writing, in addition to patterns and sounds. I might ask students to find things they think the author has done well or things they liked in the piece. They may point out conventions, like capitals for names and quotations for dialogue, but they also find words that rhyme, repeated phrases, predictable patterns, colorful adjectives and character names, italics, all capitals, bold type for emphasis, and so on. These are elements they can then put into their own writing as they see fit. I have noticed students taking the models these authors provide, and imitating them. Remember to always keep emphasis on enjoyment of the poem.

■   ■   ■   ■   ■

Morning Message. Regie Routman introduced this idea to me in her book *Invitations: Changing as Teachers and Learners K–12* Heinemann, (1991). It is another example of how meaningful communication through writing lends itself to teaching and learning about what writers do. Before school each day, I write a meaningful message on a small, portable chalkboard. I write the message in letter form and address it to students. Students and I read and discuss the message. It often contains information about upcoming events or asks questions relevant to students. After discussing the message, we look for things we know. Students point out patterns used to help them read the message. These may be on the Wall or pulled from memory. They often provide analogous words for found patterns and we write these beside the message. We note conventions, such as how the date, greeting, body, and closing of the letter are written. Students recognize capitals, end marks, and commas. They note my use of hyphens and carats. They comment on my sentence structure and my word choices. As we note each item, we circle it and quickly discuss it. Usually students have more things to note in the message than we want to take time to

review. After three or four minutes, I invite students to turn to their neighbor and share their finding. Thus, all students have the opportunity to verbalize about what they see that they know. Note how the students are mentioning things from the message that they also notice in many varied sources like the new favorite poem and the Daily News. Therefore they are constantly reviewing skills and strategies within authentic contexts. After we discuss the message, we place it in the Message Center for further use.

Throughout the school year, students may also have the opportunity to construct the Morning Message in pairs or groups. We use their writing just as we use the messages I write. We look for things we know or things that have been done well. The format of the Morning Message may be varied to present students with models of different forms of writing.

Also, the Morning Message is primarily an oral activity, while the News is written with students and may even be recorded by volunteers. The activities are alike in important ways. They are both positive models for students. I do not consciously make errors when I write the Morning Message or the News. (Students do sometimes spot and help correct unintentional errors!) But I strive to present positive models rather than focus the activity on fixing errors. Both contain interesting material related to the students or their own experiences. Instead of reviewing patterns, conventions, or elements of style through drill or direct instruction, modeling takes place through real, purposeful communication. My students love both activities. They hurry into class in the morning to read the Message, and they are always anxious to contribute to the News. As long as the activities are kept short, students will always be enthusiastic participants.

■　　■　　■　　■　　■

Reading and Writing Centers. Each day, students spend roughly fifteen minutes involved in center activities. Groups rotate to centers on a daily basis. Students are not grouped according to ability. Rather, groups for center activities are mixed. We have four centers, one in each corner of the room. Each is designed to complement the activities we are doing together in class and provide students with independent practice. There are many reading and writing choices and materials in each center.

The Morning Message is different from the Daily News because it is written before students read and examine it. The message may come only from the teacher, whereas the content of the News comes directly from the students.

■   ■   ■   ■   ■

Big Book, Poster, and Poetry Center. This center is comprised of the big books we have previously explored during shared reading, innovations produced by our class in big book form, favorite poems written on posters, our shared writing, and sentence strips from our reading strategy lessons. Students may choose what they would like to read and how they will read while in the center. They may read with a partner or group, or individually, aloud or silently. Students use pointers to track the print as they read. Post-it notes are also available for pointing out things they like, conventions, rhyming words, patterns, and so on.

The rereading of self-selected materials in this center develops fluency as well as enjoyment. I have watched the expressive choral reading that occurs, the cooperative work and strategy use, and the imitation of teacherlike behaviors as students read sentence strips and big books. The types of skills, strategies, and elements of writing we bring up in our whole-class lessons and readings are noted. Students feel empowered as readers.

■   ■   ■   ■   ■

Message Center. Our Daily News is posted here throughout the year, and this is also where children continue to use the Morning Message. Students reread the Daily News, tracking the print with pointers and using Post-its as they do in the Big Book, Poster, and Poetry Center. They may use chalk to continue to circle things they know in the Morning Message, and they can add more analogous words to the chunks they find. They may also use the back of the portable chalkboard to add their own message, again circling things they know they write.

We also have a message board on which students post messages for the class (Burke, 1988). These are shared at the end of the day. I post important communication here, including sign-up sheets for class or school activities. The mailboxes are another important feature in this center. Students are free to compose mail for one another. A mail carrier delivers student mail during the last few minutes of class.

■　　■　　■　　■　　■

Listening Center. Many teachers use listening centers in their classrooms. This is a place where students may listen to books on tape and read along. I like to expose students to new titles in this center, placing listening books in the classroom library after each group has had the chance to read them. Students are encouraged to read out loud with the tape.

We use commercially prepared tapes as well as tapes I prepare myself. On my own tapes, I often record the story using the cloze technique. I read along and stop on certain words or phrases, allowing students to fill them in. I encourage use of the chunks in the words by pronouncing the first sound in a word, leaving the rime to be read by the students. This gives them practice in how words are broken up, using learned patterns and discovering new ones, and encourages use of context.

■　　■　　■　　■　　■

Library Center. For the last center activity, a small group of students and I meet together in the class library. We select a book to read as a group (each child has a copy), and I allow students time to pre-view. Before we begin reading, they share their predictions about the book's content, questions they have, and experiences relating to the theme. I usually start the guided reading, thinking aloud about strategies I am using to comprehend the text, including the decoding-by-analogy strategy for discovering unknown words. Then student volunteers "pop in." I take notes on reading behaviors as I observe individuals read. Many of my techniques for effective note taking have come from Marie Clay's (1979) work on the Running Record.

During our day, I try to use different types of groups (whole class, heterogeneous, and homogeneous) to add variety and allow students to model for each other. At times, these groups are assigned or they may be self-selected (as they are for literature circles). The group in the library is heterogeneous, like the other center groups. I may change center groups to allow students opportunities to work with various classmates. In the library, then, abilities range from fast, fluent readers to slow, emergent readers. Heterogeneous groups are effective in fostering helpful attitudes and behaviors toward others. In order to enable learning for everyone involved, especially in the context of a guided reading session with a mixed group, students must understand that they should not instantaneously supply unknown words for others. Instead, I emphasize that we must allow time for all readers to use their strategies in order for them to learn. If we are waiting a very long time and a student is really struggling, I do allow students to assist each other, but just giving a word is not enough. I ask, "Who can help Janet?" and volunteers assist but must then explain what strategies were used to decode the unknown word. In this way, students model for one another. This method of providing assistance transfers to other cooperative activities. Student explanations for solving reading problems are often advantageous to others. Of course, during this guided time, teachers must also fill the role of supporting readers by asking questions that promote strategy use and guiding their attempts.

We explore different authors and genres in the Library Center. Books are usually short, because center time is minimal and I only meet with each group once a week. I enjoy the opportunity to interact with the students in a small group setting, and the students naturally benefit from instruction at this level. I encourage students to come back to the titles we share in the library, checking them out for SQUIRT time or taking them home to share.

■ A Note on Management

Do they really use the time? My management system is not complicated, and it is based on a philosophy of respect. The management strategies I use for the center activities are the same applied throughout our day. The students know I respect them as readers and writers, I expect them to respect each other as such, and they should respect the time they have available to them for reading and writing activities. They sometimes complain that they are not getting enough time in Centers or Reading and Writing Workshop, so they seldom waste the time they do have. Students understand many of the activities we engage in are open and steeped in free choice. They like this freedom. But I remind them they must behave as readers and writers and make productive choices in order to maintain a high level of freedom. Students know that if we are not productive, something has to change. We often debrief after center time and workshops. We talk about how time was used, what worked well, and what we could improve on. This debriefing involves students in classroom management. When students are respected and are allowed to participate in management, they take the subject seriously and strive to do their best.

■　　■　　■　　■　　■

Shared Reading. Shared reading is an opportunity to model and utilize reading strategies with the whole class within the context of real text. We always follow our reading strategy lessons with this type of reading. For successful shared reading, each student must have visual access to the print being read. This can be achieved through the use of a big book or a whole-class text set.

The strategies discussed in the reading strategy lesson now become useful as the students and I work together to get the meaning of the story. I may think aloud, mask words with Post-its, or encourage students to verbalize about their own strategy use as we proceed. I always invite the class to read along with me. When we encounter a reading problem, like the challenge word in the reading strategy sentence, we work together to solve it. We preview the book before reading, and engage in much discussion as we read. Discussions are student-centered, and they focus on relating our own experience to the text, making predictions, finding writing ideas, questioning the author, and elements of writing style. Students may also note things they know in the text as they do in other reading activities.

After my second graders have heard or chorally read a story, the print is no longer fresh. They lose the chance to use all of their strategies once the text has been shared, because they often can rely on their memory of what was read to aid problem solving in subsequent readings. So, frequently we apply our strategies to work cooperatively through the first reading of texts. True-to-life goals are another reason I never preteach vocabulary. Instead, students and I use analogy and other strategies to decode new words coupled with the context to understand these words. Naturally, teachers will also include shared reading experiences strictly for enjoyment in day-to-day activities.

After we capitalize on our strategy use during the first reading, we often revisit big books for further enjoyment. We may review strategies that were successful for us as we reread, highlighting use of decoding by analogy. We may note items for inclusion on our Help Wall. Often, open-ended class discussions take place, in which students make connections between characters, events, and other books.

In addition to shared reading with a big book, we are always in the process of reading a class novel. Each student has a copy. I bring in books written on varying reading levels. Titles we read last year in my second grade class include: *Stone Fox* by John Reynolds Gardner, *Charlotte's Web* by E.B. White, *Fantastic Mr. Fox*

> **M**any sources suggest that the first reading of a big book should be purely for enjoyment, perhaps through the teacher reading aloud to students. Enjoyment must always come first, but I do utilize many new titles as opportunities for strategy use.

by Roald Dahl, *Catwings* by Ursula LeGuin and *Hello Mrs. Piggle Wiggle* by Betty MacDonald. I often think aloud about my use of strategies as I read and students follow. I may read and pause on a word, giving students the chance to fill it in. I may say the beginning sound of a word, having students supply the chunk. After a student has read a portion of the text I will sometimes ask, "I heard you pause on this word. What strategies did you use to figure it out?" Students often report on their use of the chunks and words they know to determine a difficult word. By sharing, we make the use of that strategy known to everyone, which is especially helpful to those who may not have thought to use a particular strategy. Sharing which specific strategies work and when they work is very helpful to developing readers.

A great source for learning about shared and guided reading is Margaret Mooney's *Reading To, With, and By Children* (1990).

■   ■   ■   ■   ■

Reading Workshop. During Reading Workshop time, students have many reading options. Reading Workshop and SQUIRT provide students with the opportunity to read and explore books of different genres and on a variety of topics. The time is also used for reading Book Box books and responding in logs. Students may share their entries with others for response or revisit the Reading/Writing Centers. While students are engaged in these activities, I meet with a homogeneous reading group for a guided reading session. Of course, all of these reading activities provide students with practice in strategy use.

Sometimes we forgo our Reading Workshop time to have literature circles. Students choose a book from book sets they are interested in reading and sharing. I get students interested in the titles by giving a short book talk on each.

Multiple copies of titles by the same author are available for students to choose from. After circles of students read and discuss the books, they share with the rest of the class, exposing everyone to alternative titles by the new author. *Grand Conversations* (1990) by Ralph Peterson and Maryann Eeds is a useful resource for getting started with literature circles.

Guided Reading. Guided reading differs from shared reading in that the teacher works with a small group rather than the whole class. In my class, there are at least two guided reading sessions per day, one in the library center with a heterogeneous group and one during Reading Workshop with a homogeneous group. Students with similar reading needs can be supported and challenged within the homogeneous grouping. Group membership is flexible and changes to meet the needs of individuals. Guided reading gives students a chance to apply the reading strategies I have modeled. It also gives me opportunities to see which strategies need more modeling. I choose titles that fit the needs of a particular group. Marie Clay (1979) suggests that books are on the appropriate instructional level when students make errors only on 5 to 10 percent of the text. I need to work with students on their instructional level in order to guide and support them, stretching and improving upon their strategy use. Books in which children make fewer than 5 percent errors are too easy for guided reading (these are appropriate for success in independent reading), and books in which more than 10 percent errors are made present so many problems that comprehension can be impeded (these are books on the frustration level). Of course, these percentages are only guidelines and should not be applied to individuals in a rigid way. Running Records and other forms of individual reading assessment and observation can be used to determine appropriate books. At the beginning of the year, for example, the types and titles of books we read ranged from *There's a Wocket in My Pocket* by Dr. Seuss to *Freckle Juice* by Judy Blume in order to meet the needs of different groups of children.

We preview and discuss the book before reading. The session begins as I read, model, and talk about my strategy use, and then student volunteers "pop in." I note reading behaviors, and when problems arise, children are given the opportunity to self-correct miscues or apply different strategies before help is offered. The homogeneous groups allow me to challenge and support every student. Thus, more advanced students are not limited to second-grade books. I move ahead with them using titles that meet their needs. At the same time less developed students are not continually frustrated. Together we read titles that match this group's needs on a lower instructional level.

■　　　■　　　■　　　■　　　■

Writing Workshop. Writing Workshop is one of our favorite activities. We have a constant, sustained time for writing that everyone counts on every day. Nance Atwell's (1987) structure for Writing Workshop provides a stable, predictable format that balances instruction and modeling with adequate time for composing, sharing, and publishing.

Sometimes our Workshop begins with the Challenge Word activity as warm-up. We then re-evaluate topics added to our Writing Workshop topic list throughout the day, and students record ideas they like on individual topic lists in their writing folders. Next we have a five-to-ten minute minilesson. During this time we discuss procedures for the workshop. They might include where publishing materials are located, how to peer-conference, and when to turn in a piece for teacher-editing. Minilessons also address skills and strategies students may use as writers and issues about writing craft and style. Modeled writing typically occurs during minilessons as well.

Modeled writing, in this case, is different from other related techniques described in the Daily News and the Morning Message. I learned about this type of writing in the Early Literacy Inservice Course (ELIC) offered in a neighboring district. Instead of just thinking aloud about strategies and use of conventions while writing a short message, I also demonstrate my own writing process in its entirety. This type of modeled writing is the key to providing students with a concrete model of what real writers do. And they can learn writing conventions. The modeled writing approach is the only method I have found that actually works for student revision. The only catch is (and this is a good catch) the teacher is the model! You have to become involved in writing for your own purpose, and you have to be willing to share it with students. But you might be surprised with the results. You will see changes in your students' writing, and perhaps in yourself as a writer, too.

Chart paper works well for my draft during modeled writing. First I think aloud how I may generate a variety of writing topics. I show how I evaluate my ideas, choose one, and move on to prewriting. I usually model how I take writer's notes as events and ideas come to mind related to my chosen topic. Then I talk aloud about using my notes to begin composing a piece. As I write, I model appropriate strategy use. I use analogy to quickly invent spellings. I reread parts I have written, evaluating my word choices and referring to my thesaurus or other class reference lists. I add, delete, and revise. Students see how I get stumped, need to conference with someone, and how I put my writing aside, coming back to it another day. When my piece is complete, I may choose to publish it in a book, class anthology, or on a poster. I model many writing genres throughout the year, thereby exposing students to varied possibilities for their own writing.

> *Through modeled writing, students can learn about the recursive nature of the writing process. They can learn how to craft their own style of writing. They learn about "the challenges writers face, the options open to them, and how they make decisions" (Wilkinson, 1990, 18).*

Modeled writing of this sort takes place over a number of days, though the minilesson lasts only five to ten minutes. I simply continue writing in front of students the next day.

After the minilesson, our class has silent writing time. I added this section to our Writing Workshop schedule because I wanted time to write. I do not model writing during the Workshop minilesson everyday. But, by writing during silent time, I do provide the students with a model of teacher-as-writer each day. It is important for students to see that I value what I ask them to do, and I do those same things myself. Also, silent writing time ensures that students are working on their own individual pieces, while perhaps using other Workshop time to work on cooperative writing.

Silent writing time lasts three or four minutes and is followed by open Workshop time. Students are free to share their writing with peers, ask questions, and work on cooperative pieces, using the time  to work through their own writing process. They may also edit their work, circling things they have done well and fixing mistakes, using the "Things I Know When I Write" strategy (Wagstaff, 1993). They further use this time to publish their work in a variety of ways. Time for writing is gradually built up as the year proceeds. My students can easily write for twenty-five minutes or more.

I use open time to conference with students. Sometimes I assemble a small group with similar writing needs; however, most writing conferences are individual. Conferencing is an ideal time to comment on the content of a student's work (I always speak about the content first) and to model and support the use of strategies. When focusing on strategies, I compliment students on their use of patterns to develop logical invented spellings. We may analyze a few of their attempts and work to refine their strategy use. The same is true for all strategies I see students using as writers. I first compliment their approximations and proper uses, then help them improve. Students add the conventional spellings of some words that they feel are important to their dictionaries. I keep notes on the writing behaviors students are developing in their drafts and on the strategies I quickly model or help them with during this one-on-one session.

During individual conferences my total attention is focused on the student at hand. The rest know they should rely on each other for help rather than interrupt a conference. Students may sign their name on the board for help, and I meet with them when my scheduled conferences are over. On alternating workshop days, I make myself available to everyone during open time. I am thus able to respond to and assist students, which helps their writing improve.

Writing Workshop concludes with class sharing time (often referred to as "Author's Chair"). Sharing time allows students to orally "publish" writing and involves them in responding. Through sharing, writers are exposed to endless possibilities, including topic ideas, genres, styles, and publishing options. Hearing the work of others stretches my students' imaginations and undoubtedly improves their writing.

When a student shares a piece, the class gives three positive comments or "hearts," and one idea or "wish." Writers know they have the option of incorporating the wish into their writing or ignoring it. Students maintain control over their writing at all times. I start the year by modeling appropriate response techniques, and students quickly take over. The responding that occurs during class sharing time carries over to peer sharing during open workshop time.

Donald Graves's book *Writing: Teachers and Children At Work* (1983) has given me many super ideas for running a successful Writing Workshop and has helped me to improve my conferencing techniques.

■   ■   ■   ■   ■

SQUIRT (Sustained, quiet, uninterrupted, individual reading time). As previously mentioned, SQUIRT provides students with a large chunk of quality self-guided reading time. They need this time in order to access the many titles of interest in our classroom. Time available gradually increases as students' capacity to use it grows. During many SQUIRT sessions, I read silently with the class. At other times, I hold individual reading conferences. At the beginning of the year, I have students read to me and I complete a Running Record (Clay, 1979). The Running Record helps me get an idea of how students are reading and what strategies they are or are not developing. As the year progresses, I periodically meet to formally assess reading growth and strategy use again. Of course, I look for how students are using decoding by analogy along with other complementary strategies. At other times, I meet with individuals to discuss and interact with their reading selection. As students read to or with me, I model, question, analyze, and stretch strategy use as I do during individual writing conferences. These meetings allow me to become very familiar with students' reading preferences. I use this knowledge to guide the selection of books I make available in our class library. In addition, I can encourage students to explore different authors and genres by using information from reading conferences.

The philosophy that guides the methods I use to help students develop literate behaviors is quite simple. I continually remind myself that I want to use methods that treat students as real readers and writers, so I only teach skills and strategies they can actually use in reading and writing. These are usually the strategies I use myself.

Clay, M.M. (1979). *The early detection of reading difficulties.*
New Zealand: Heinemann Education.
Graves, D. H. (1983). *Writing: Teachers and children at work,*
Portsmouth, NH: Heinemann.
Harste, J.C., Short, K.G., and Burke, C. (1988). *Creating classrooms for authors: The reading-writing connection.* Portsmouth, NH: Heinemann.
Mooney, M.E. (1990). *Reading to, with, and by children,* Katonah, NY:
Richard C. Owen Publishers, Inc.
Peterson, R. &Eeds, M. (1990) *Grand Conversations: Literature groups in action.*
New York: Scholastic Inc.
Routman, R. (1991). *Invitations: Changing as teachers and learners K-12.*
Postmouth, NH: Heinemann.
Wagstaff, J. (1993). Writing Skills. *Instructor,* 102, 52.
Wilkinson. L. (1990). Modeled writing. *Early Literacy Inservice Course Unit 9: Teaching writing.* (pp. 12-18). Crystal Lake, IL: Rigby.

Student Progress

My class consisted of twenty-eight second graders of varied abilities from an economically mixed, predominantly middle class suburban area. Their work shows evidence of how these strategies can bring success and empowerment to readers and writers.

The prospect of sharing my students' progress is exciting yet astounding. Looking over their drafts from September through June, their reading logs and assessments, learning logs and journals, I am overwhelmed with information. Every student made interesting gains last year. Here is the payoff for all the effort! Every student shows evidence of using the analogy strategies. I only wish I could share more of their work.

As you read my descriptions, you will notice references to the use of Word Wall patterns. When I speak of Word Wall patterns, I mean that the rime has been taught, not necessarily that the student is referring directly to the Wall. Student work also shows evidence of the use of many patterns beyond the Wall. Changes shown occurred as a matter of analogy instruction, students' own discovery of analogies in their reading and writing, and the strategies learned and experiences gained in and beyond our total program.

Unfortunately, most of the first available writing samples are from a few weeks into the school year. So, many of these samples (with the exception of Brett's) are not true representations of what most students were doing before exposure to patterns and the analogy ideas. I was so excited about trying the strategies that I began modeling them in the first few days of school. If I had earlier samples, writing progress would be even more evident.

As you examine the writing samples, a few things may catch your attention. Names have been deleted to assure anonymity. So, you will see gaps in the writing. You will also note how students have made revisions in the form of scribbles and circled and identified things they have done well as writers. Please look beyond our "sloppy copies" (all samples are drafts) to see the exciting progress the samples depict.

■ Looking Closely at Two Students

Because I cannot share the progress of every student, I would like to look closely at the work of two students who started the year on or below grade level and made striking gains.

JOHN

John began the year reading at the first-grade instructional level as assessed on an informal reading inventory (Sucher-Allred, 1981). Given a first-grade passage containing eighty-eight words, he made seven miscues. His reading was characterized as slow and laborious. According to my analysis of his errors, he seemed to be using initial visual cues to quickly predict words, ignoring both meaning and patterns. Many errors resulted that were not structurally or meaningfully consistent with the passage. For example, on one occasion John slowly read, "One *everything,* Father Goat asked, 'Has *only* seen my cap?'" for "One *evening,* Father Goat asked, 'Has *anyone* seen my cap?'" Consequently, John's comprehension suffered. Some of John's miscues on the reading inventory included reading *car* for *care,* and *trouble* for *tough.* I concluded that John could use strategies that would help him attend to the patterns in words. Attention to the visual cues in the patterns would move him beyond the initial sounds in words. He also needed strategies that would encourage the use of context clues and self-checking for meaning, as he frequently made errors that interrupted the meaning of the text but read on without noticing them.

John's needs demonstrate how important it is for students to learn strategies for using all cues available to them including the graphophonic, semantic, and syntactic. The minilessons and instruction in decoding by analogy help promote the quick, efficient phonetic cues, while attention to all strategies during the reading strategy lessons and guided and shared reading foster the use of all cues in combination. My goal is to help develop well-balanced readers who are able to exploit all necessary information to get at meaning and who can rely on themselves to do so.

By mid-November, John's reading had improved dramatically. He already showed evidence of using patterns to move beyond initial cues and guessing. For example, when retested on the reading inventory, he correctly read multisyllabic words on the third-grade word list and in the corresponding passage. He read *hospital,* reporting that he had looked for the chunks to see *hos, pit,* and *al.* He paused on the words *strapped, strike,* and *balcony,* correctly reading each. When asked about these words, he said, "I got them when I looked at the chunks." By comparison, these words seem more difficult than the words John was miscuing on in September.

In a third-grade passage with 147 words, he made only seven miscues, which would indicate that the passage was at his instructional level. He self-corrected two errors to maintain meaning. Other miscues were much more consistent with the meaning of the passage than his September errors. For example, John read, "Up in the cabin his father saw a *flash* of light," when the sentence actually said, "Up in the cabin his father saw the *flashes* of light." These errors are minor, and they maintain meaning. When viewed in combination with the way John was now attacking words, one could say he was developing a more balanced use of strategies. I observed these developments in guided reading sessions as well, noting an increase in fluency, expression, self-correcting for meaning, and pattern use. As mentioned, I often ask my students to explain their strategy use when I notice them pausing and examining words. This self-reporting helps me to get a glimpse of what students are thinking, and it supports other readers as well. John paused while reading *explained* in a guided session. When he finished reading, I asked how he had figured out the word. He said, "I saw *ain* like in *rain* (*rain* was on the Word Wall), I knew *ex* 'cause I see it all the time. So, I knew it was *explained*." On another occasion he explained how he decoded the word *empty*, "I saw *em* like *them* and *ty* like *twenty*." John was already comfortable with decoding by analogy, understanding when and how to use it. Attention to patterns coupled with meaning was paying off for him. He was now enjoying books more, talking to others about what he was reading, and sharing favorites at home. His comprehension was greatly increased by relying less on predicting using only initial sounds. John's self-confidence as a reader was improving.

By the end of the school year, John was reading fluently on the fourth grade level. I asked him to read a fourth grade passage with 166 words to me. He made only three miscues! My Running Record shows he was rereading for sense, self-correcting errors, and using wonderful expression. On the fourth- and fifth-grade word lists, he was decoding words like *deflector, exhibited,* and *candidates,* reporting, for example, "I saw *can* like *an* from *pan,* I saw *did,* and then *ates* like *hates*." John was decoding by analogy using words from memory. None of the words he knew in the above case were key words from the Wall. Even errors made on these word lists show pattern use. John read *magic can* for *magician* on the fifth-grade list. Had this word been embedded in context, as it is in real reading, perhaps he would have decoded the word correctly.

John's ability to better solve reading problems affected his love for reading. He became increasingly more involved in our book shares, and his attitude toward his own abilities greatly improved. He emerged as a leader in literature circles and open-ended discussions, whereas he would withdraw from many of these activities before. On a written survey his mother commented, "John did not comprehend what he read (before). If he read a word incorrectly, he was not aware of it. Now he is able to correct his mistakes and make sense of his reading." John became a better self-checker as he read, fixing miscues in search of meaning. The analogy strategy gave him a tool for dealing with larger words, and for attending to the chunks to help him fix errors. Additionally, attention to rimes helped him move beyond initial cues.

In writing, John made similar improvements using analogy. In

FIGURE 4

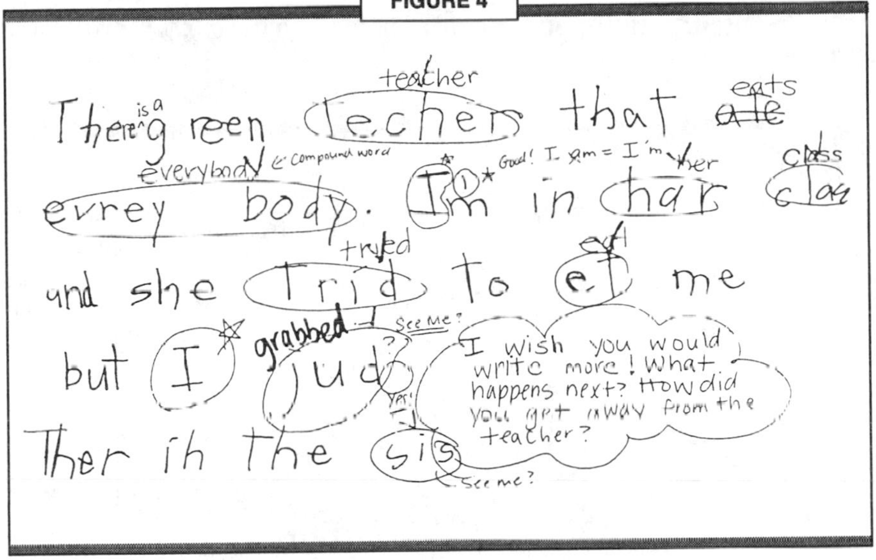

Ther is a green teacher that eats everybody. I'm in har class and she trid to et me but I jud Ther in the sis

(Teacher annotations: teacher, eats, is a, everybody & Compound word, Good! I am = I'm, her, class, tryed, et, grabbed, See me?, I wish you would write more! What happens next? How did you get away from the teacher?, See me?)

September, his invented spellings included *har* for *her*, *et* for *eat*, *jud* for *grabbed* and *sis* for *shins* (see fig. 4). He was obviously making some use of his letter-sound correspondence knowledge, but he showed little evidence of spelling pattern awareness. He often had to help me read his attempts to decipher them for publishing. Notice in the later samples how the use of patterns positively influences his invented spellings. They become much more sophisticated and true to sound, and the number of correctly spelled words in John's compositions dramatically increases. By January, he wrote *befor* for *before* (using the *or* pattern from the Word Wall word *for*), *thay* for *they* (using the first rime in the Word Wall word *playground*) and *nocken* for *knockin'* (using *ock* from *sock*) (see Fig. 5). His conventional spellings include *last, night, robbers, door,* and *corn,* among many others, all of which have patterns from the Wall. John was writing much more confidently, increasing the length of his stories as he gained ease in spelling. The September sample (Fig. 5) includes only twenty-three words, eight of which are misspelled. In that piece, John's spelling was approximately 65 percent accurate. In comparison, the January sample has fifty-two words, 92 percent of which are spelled correctly. By using pattern and listening for chunks, John created inventions that became increasingly logical and easy for the reader to understand. Whereas in September his spellings indicated the ability to hear and encode initial and final sounds, in January he was encoding all word parts. Assuredly, involvement in constant writing also promoted spelling growth.

FIGURE 5

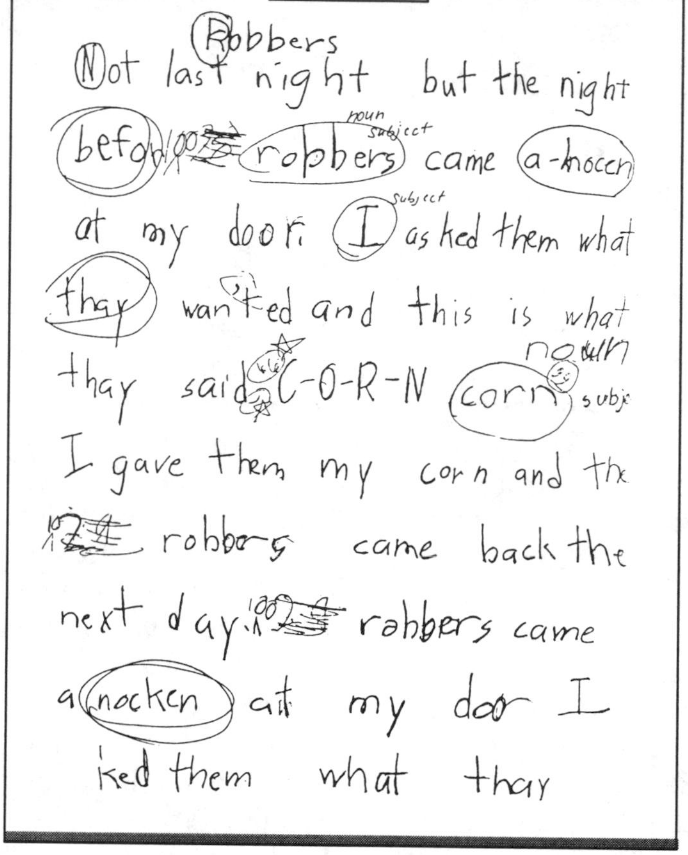
Robbers
Not last night but the night
before robbers came a-knocen
at my door. I asked them what
thay wanted and this is what
thay said C-O-R-N corn
I gave them my corn and the
robbers came back the
next day robbers came
a nocken at my door I
ked them what thay

An April reading log entry (fig. 6) demonstrates John's continued pattern use for invented spellings. Again, he wrote *thay* for *they.* This is a good invented attempt, but as a common word, the pattern of John's misspelling sent up a red flag. I spoke with John about this misspelling and encouraged him to slow down and use the Help Wall or his dictionary to develop the habit of spelling this word correctly. Looking back, I feel I can emphasize the correct spelling of such words even more in my instruction, perhaps using a few more of Cunningham's (1991) activities to encourage the development of better habits. John produced other logical inventions in this piece, including *indein* for *indian, frends* for *friends,* and *blud* for *blood.* If you look at the way *in de in* was written, you can see how John is listening for word parts to break up the spelling task and apply patterns. I see this in several children's writing. I interpret it as evidence that listening for chunks and applying patterns makes sense to students as they invent spellings.

Lastly, take a look at a few of John's short journal entries from May (fig. 7). I note only one invented spelling. *Sochool* was written for *school*. He may have used the *ool* pattern from the Wall, or perhaps he recalled it from words in his memory. Whatever the case, I know it says *school*. I'm pleased that his invented spellings make sense and that he is becoming more and more conventional. His samples show a continual pattern of growth.

John's mother agrees. In December, when asked to comment on John's midyear progress, she wrote, "As a writer, John is showing much more enthusiasm and writes stories and poems that he has never done before at home. As a speller, John has come a long way. Not all words are spelled correctly, but I see more and more words correct and it seems to be much easier and makes more sense to him."

I recorded an interview I had with John on his strategy use at the end of the school year. I asked him how he felt when he came to words he didn't know while reading and what he did about those words. He said, "I use the chunks." I asked him when he used that

FIGURE 7

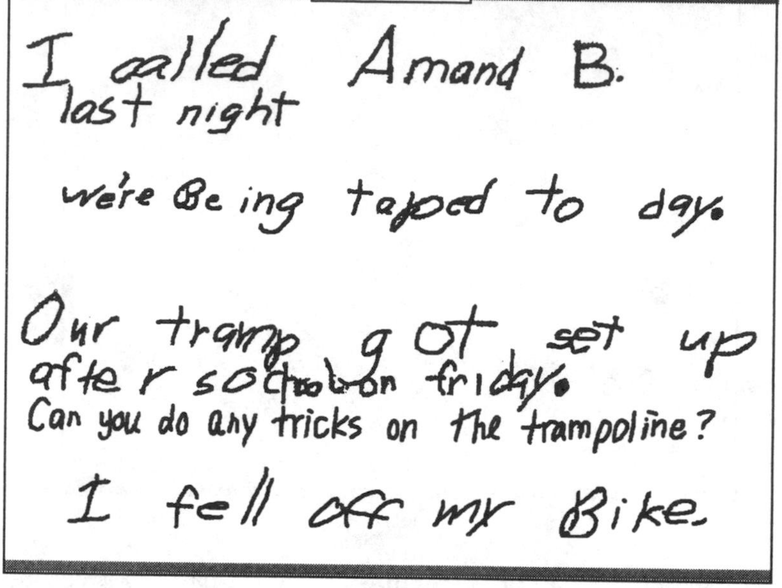

> I called Amand B.
> last night
>
> we're Being taped to day.
>
> Our tramp got set up
> after soc hool on friday.
> Can you do any tricks on the trampoline?
>
> I fell off my Bike.

strategy, and he replied, "Most of the time." He added that using the patterns to read "makes things easier." When asked whether "big" words made him nervous and what he did to deal with them, he reported that looking for the chunks in long words made it easy. He even pointed to a multisyllabic word on a page of text in front of us and showed me. "This is *punishment*. It's easy to see the chunks. There is *pun, un* like *fun, ish* like *fish,* and *ment* like *apartment.*"

I followed up by asking what he does to write long words he doesn't know how to spell with certainty. He answered, "I see if I can write it, and if I don't get it right, then I listen for the chunks." Obviously, John uses analogy, the strategies make sense for him, and because he comments so freely about them, those strategies have been responsible for some of his growth.

HILLARY

Hillary began the year reading on grade level according to her informal reading inventory. On the word recognition lists and in the passages, she used sounding out letter-by-letter as a strategy for attacking unfamiliar words. She was unable to read many of the words on the second grade midyear list, missing nine out of twenty.

At times she began to sound out a word and gave up midstream or guessed the ending. She was unable to read words like *funniest, suppose, canyons, treasures, salad,* and *announcer.* When she read connected text, she used the same attack plan. Her sounding-out strategy often led her to misread words. Like John, she was not self-checking for meaning. With instruction in decoding by analogy in combination with syntactic and semantic strategies, improvement was quickly evident. After a few weeks, I noted how Hillary used patterns to decode the words *Anthony* and *corvette* in a guided reading session with the book *Alexander and the Horrible, Terrible, No Good, Very Bad Day* by Judith Viorst. In reading both words, she literally broke them into their parts, reading *An thon y,* and *cor vette.* Based on my notes about her reading behaviors just weeks earlier, I believe it had never occurred to her to attack words by attending to larger pieces rather than individual letters.

In November, I retested Hillary. Her reading level had jumped, enabling her to read the fourth-grade passage on an independent level. In the 166-word story, she made only five miscues! She was able to retell what had happened in the story with ease. Her miscues on the word tests showed attention to patterns. She misread *structure* as *strucker, deflector* as *delector,* and *knowledge* as *no ledge.* She no longer simply gave up after beginning to sound out words. Instead, her attention now seemed to be geared to all word parts. She read the second-grade and third-grade word lists with few errors, reading all words she had miscued in September with ease. On the fourth-grade list, she missed only three words. It's compelling to compare that number to the nine missed on the second-grade list two months earlier.

Additionally, at the time of the November inventory, Hillary was consciously aware of her strategy use; reporting, for example, that she saw *dis* like *miss* and *ance* like *dance* to decode *distance.* This case shows how she was using the strategy in a flexible manner, because she used the approximate spelling of the rime *iss* to decode *is* in the first syllable *dis.* Assuredly, her strategies still needed to be refined, familiarity with new patterns needed to be built (like *ture* in *structure* from the miscue above), and emphasis on meaning required more development. But these were large gains for such a short period.

Parent comments from December revealed that Hillary relied

heavily on decoding by analogy because it worked well for her. She used patterns at home from the Word Wall at school. Her father wrote, "Hillary frequently sounds out many words when she reads aloud. Many times this year she explained to me that she looked for chunks from other words she knew." He went on to cite examples stating, "For *undignified,* she first saw *dig,* then broke it down into *un dig nif ied.* She recognized *ion* and associated it with the word *lotion* to read *position.* For *relaxed,* she identified *ax,* and knew how to pronounce the *ed* saying, "That is in a lot of my other words." He further remarked about Hillary's newfound excitement and appetite for reading, telling of the ease with which she was reading third-grade books from recommended reading lists at the local library. Commenting on her achievements from the first of the school year he wrote, "The most obvious improvement is the fluency of reading stories aloud. She hesitates less often and for shorter times to identify hard words."

When Hillary was assessed again in May, her reading skills were continuing to advance. This only confirmed what I already knew from observations during guided reading sessions: she was becoming more fluent with difficult text. Now she read books written on fourth- and fifth-grade levels fluently, presenting very few reading problems. On a sixth-grade passage from the reading inventory, Hillary made only three miscues! Because the story had 185 words, Hillary had read at the independent level! The words she had difficulty with were *Olympic* and *abreast.* For *abreast,* she first tried *a breast,* pronouncing the rime *east* like *feast.* Because that didn't make sense, she tried *abreezed.* I then told Hillary the word and explained the meaning in the passage. *Olympic* and *abreast* don't contain frequent patterns and presented problems based on the fact that Hillary, as a second grader, had little familiarity with these words, given her background experience. Therefore, the context was not extremely helpful. In fact, the whole passage, which was about an Olympic 400-meter relay race, included information that was new. Still, Hillary was able to read fluently and understand and retell what she had read.

Of course, on the word lists, Hillary did equally well. She read sixth-grade words like *disaster* with ease, breaking them up *(dis as ter)* as before. The few miscues she made showed reliance on patterns, as when she read *soot* as *suit* (like the pattern in *boot).*

In writing, Hillary began the year with more skills than John, but her invented spellings in September varied widely from almost correct to way off the mark. Samples of her attempts in varied writing settings follow. These demonstrate her need for improvement. Her learning log from September included: *wot* for *want,* *charch* for *charge,* and *hous* for *house.* In a composition dated September 14, Hillary invented *prs* for *hers,* *bresfit* for *breakfast,* and *hloe* for *hello.* In a reading log entry from late September, she wrote *fily* for *finally* and *esy* for *easy* (fig. 8). She fared better with *becuse* for *because, ception* for *kept on,* and *meny* for *many.* An analysis of these early attempts reveals that Hillary was making use of letter-sounds to create spellings, but as the year progressed and her familiarity with sounds of rimes grew, her ability to create better inventive spellings became clear.

FIGURE 8

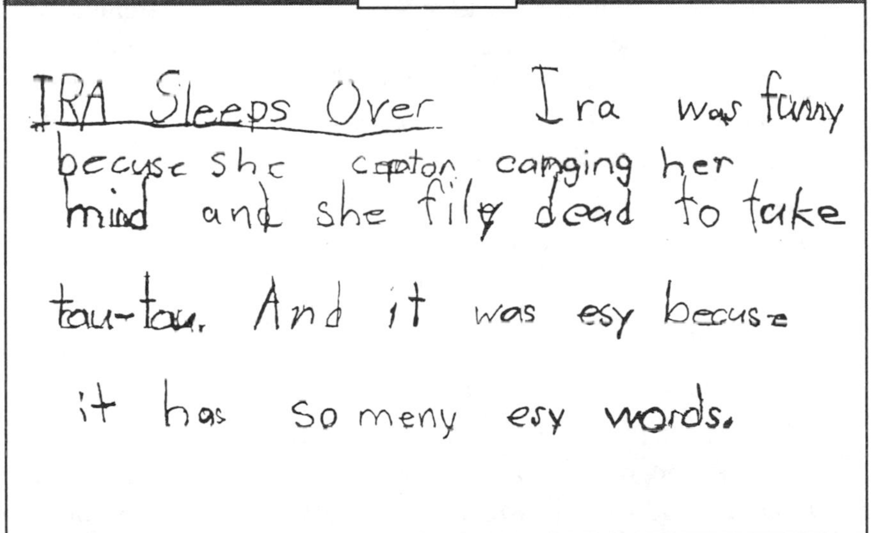

IRA Sleeps Over   Ira was funny becuse she ception camging her mind and she fily dead to take tau-tau. And it was esy becuse it has so meny esy words.

Just as Hillary was making amazing, quick gains in reading, the same was true in her writing. By November, her invented spellings showed increasing use of patterns, resulting in more attempts that were easily deciphered. She wrote: *dus* for *does* (using the pattern in the Word Wall word *bus*), *monny* for *money, perents* for *parents,* and *rite* for *right* (using the Word Wall word *kite*) (see fig. 9). Not only had her inventions improved, but her proportion of correct spellings had skyrocketed from approximately 70 percent in September samples to 93 percent in her story "New Shoes," which she composed in November.

Hillary became comfortable inventing spellings for much harder words. Samples from the Challenge Word activity demonstrate how she accomplished this through the use of patterns. She tried *avencher* (using Word Wall patterns: *en* from *ten* and *er* from *her)* for *adventure, prisiners* for *prisoners,* and *activety (ive* like *give* and *ty* like *twenty)* for *activity.* Note here how Hillary's invented spellings are affected by how accurately she hears the words she is trying to spell (as in *avencher).* This seems to be true for most of my students. As they develop increased awareness of the pronunciation of words and their vocabulary increases, their inventions become more accurate.

In December her dad wrote, "Hillary has done a lot more writing this year than ever before. She really seems to enjoy writing poems and notes to friends or family. Prior to this year, I don't think she felt confident enough to try writing complete letters and sharing them with others…Her spelling is often done phonetically, not always accurate, but very well executed. I have been very pleased with her writing efforts."

Hillary's father attributed her new confidence to the analogy strategy, stating, "I have noticed Hillary using word chunks in her writing. This skill is probably a key reason she writes so confidently. She rarely hesitates to phonetically attempt words based on word chunks she already knows. I recently asked her how she knew how to correctly spell the word *starlight.* She said that *star* was easy and *ight* sounded the same as it did in *tonight.*"

Hillary's accuracy did increase during the year, thus addressing her father's concern. But the confidence she gained as a writer by using patterns and analogy was even more exciting for me to observe. Now Hillary had more tools to further ignite her passion for learning. The analogy strategy appeared to help her achieve a new level of success, and she found writing easier. I was confident that she would continue to develop, moving more toward conventional spelling, now that she was writing so prolifically.

In February, Hillary's obvious use of patterns persisted, the words she attempted were more difficult, and her percentage of correct words held steady at a rate of 90 percent or better. Figure 10

FIGURE 9

New Shoes

New shoes are very fun to get when your old ones wear~ [were] out* Sometimes you want new shoes when you don't need them* Sometimes your mom or dad does [dus] not have the money~ [monny] to get them and you hare to go with out them* Sometimes your parents~ [perents] will get them Whenever [when ever] you want* When you get new shoes you have to find the right [rite] size* And [And] the ones you love* The end

FIGURE 10

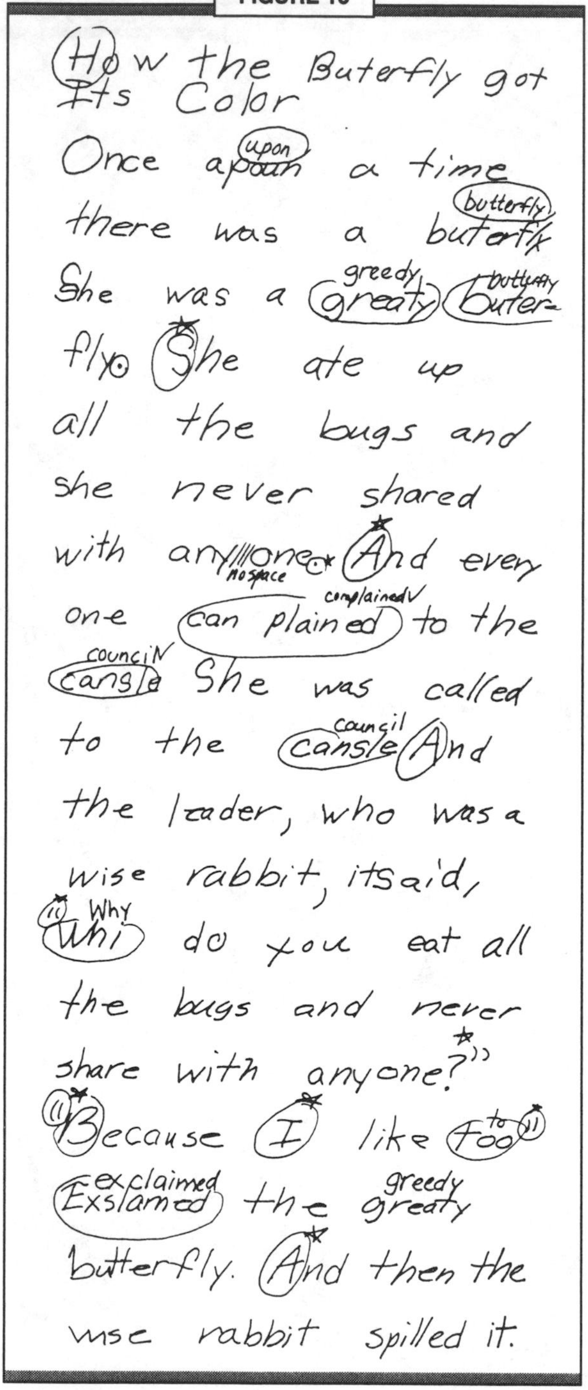

How the Buterfly got
Its Color

Once apoun [upon] a time
there was a buterfly [butterfly]
She was a greaty [greedy] buter- [butterfly]
fly. She ate up
all the bugs and
she never shared
with anyone. [no space] And every
one can plained [complained] to the
cansle [councin] She was called
to the cansle [council] And
the leader, who was a
wise rabbit, it said,
Why [Whi] do you eat all
the bugs and never
share with anyone?"
"Because I like too [to]
exslamed [exclaimed] the greaty [greedy]
buterfly. And then the
wise rabbit spilled it.

shows great inventive spellings: *greaty* (*eat* as in *treat*) for *greedy,*
buterfly for *butterfly, cun plained* for *complained, exslamed* (*ame* as
in *game*) for *exclaimed,* and *cansle* for *council.* I must point out here
again how the break in the word *complained,* as Hillary wrote it, indi-
cates the way she was listening for the chunks, hearing breaks, and
encoding new spellings from the rimes in known words (*cun* is like
the Word Wall word *fun* and *plained* has the rime from *rain*). Correct
spellings from February's "How the Butterfly Got Its Color" include
beautiful, because, paint, everyone and *stain.* Hillary was misspelling
much easier words back in September.

The icing on the cake comes when you look at Hillary's later
rough draft samples. Figure 11 from April and figure 12 from May
show how well Hillary had mastered patterns and had moved toward
conventional spellings. In both drafts Hillary made very few errors. In
April she wrote *breath* for *breathe* in two cases, but also wrote the
word correctly in two other cases. She miscoded *olny* for *only* and
wrote *droped* for *dropped.* In May she encoded *biulding* for *building*
and wrote *whide* for *wide.* Every other word was correct! Notice how
she conventionally wrote words like *squeaked, caught, because,* and
believe (fig. 11) and *awesome, lawyer,* and *gorilla* (fig. 12). Hillary
obviously had moved beyond reliance on the Wall. She used patterns
only when necessary to invent spellings logically, as when she wrote
culection for *collection* in her journal on May 6. I'm sure Hillary's
father is very proud of how she is spelling now. These great spelling
achievements can be attributed to many factors, of which analogy and
automaticity with patterns are certainly two.

My interview with Hillary at the end of the year confirmed the
fact that she was conscientious about her strategy use. She remarked,
"Looking for the chunks makes reading better. You don't have to skip
words so you don't get the story. You try to use the chunks." When
asked about long, multisyllabic words Hillary said, "If it's just a long
word that you don't really get, then it's easy to use the chunks." I next
asked Hillary to read a challenging word she hadn't seen before from
a sixth-grade list. The word was *generations.* She read it accurately
stating, "I see *gen* like *pen, er* like *her, a,* and *tion* like *lotion.* Then I
just added *s.*" Hillary is another example of a student who demonstrates in-depth understanding and easy use of the analogy strategies.

FIGURE 11

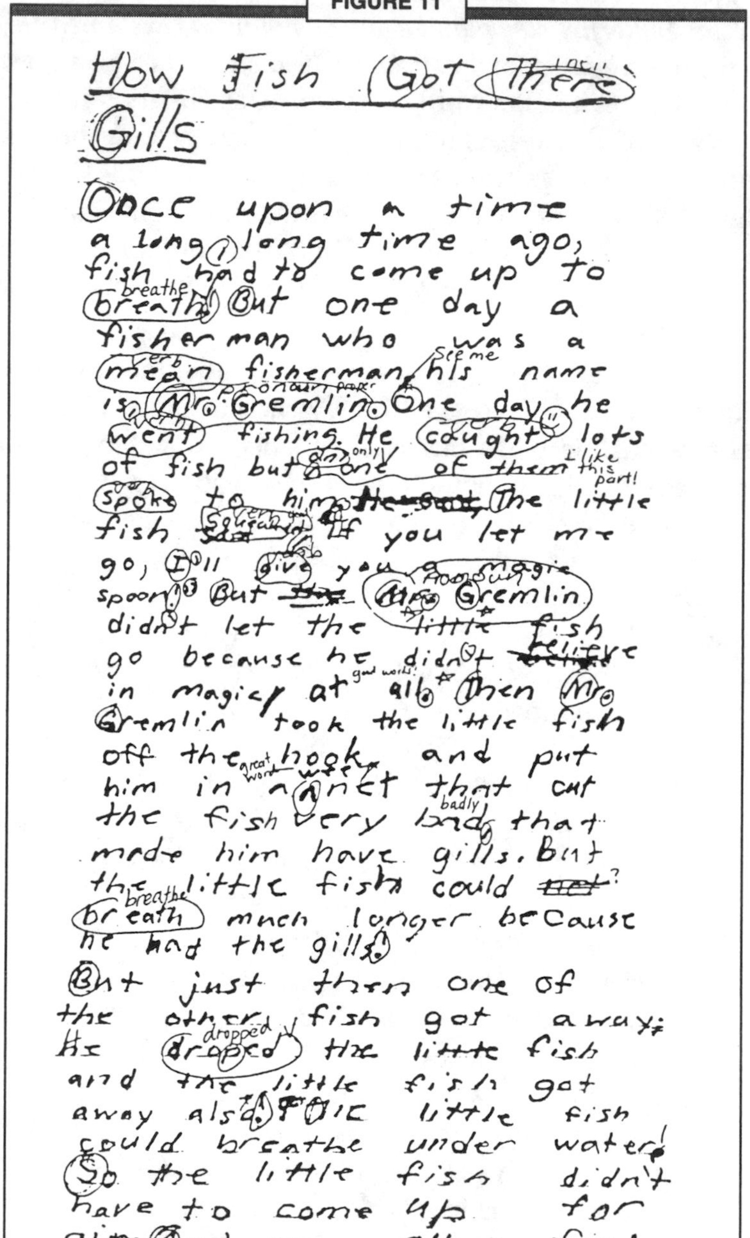

How Fish (Got there) Gills

Once upon a time a long long time ago, fish had to come up to breath. But one day a fisherman who was a mean fisherman, his name is Mr. Gremlin. One day he went fishing. He caught lots of fish but only one of them spoke to him. The little fish said, "If you let me go, I'll give you a magic spoon." But Mr. Gremlin didn't let the little fish go because he didn't believe in magic at all. Then Mr. Gremlin took the little fish off the hook, and put him in a net that cut the fish very badly that made him have gills. But the little fish could breath much longer because he had the gills.

But just then one of the other fish got away. He dropped the little fish and the little fish got away also. The little fish could breathe under water! So the little fish didn't have to come up for air. And now all fish, and all kinds of fish, have gills and are able to breathe in water.

FIGURE 12

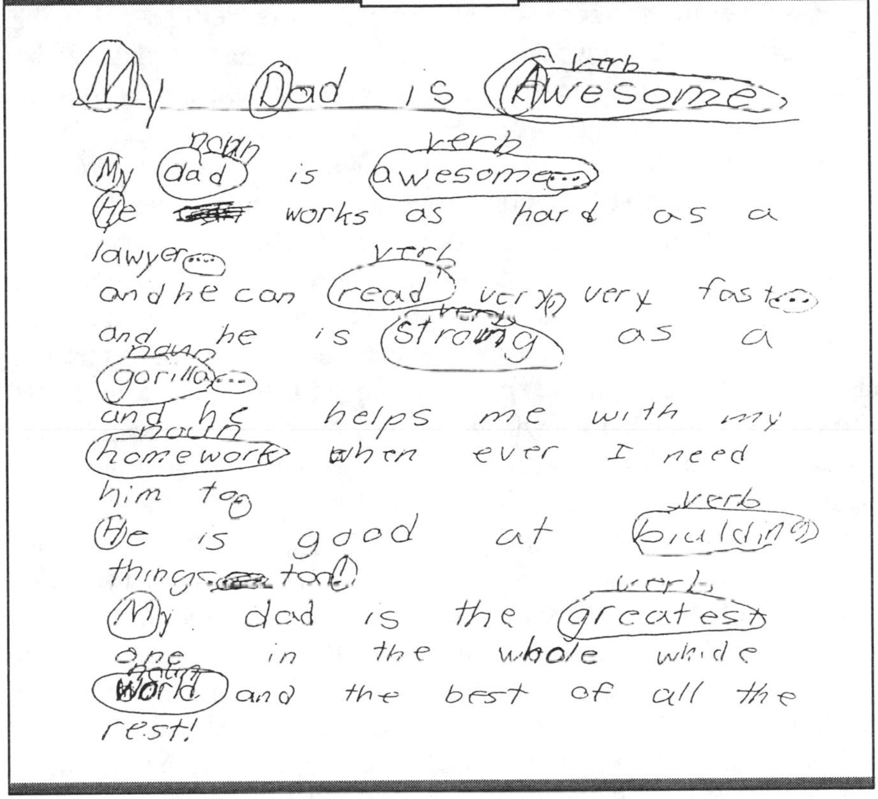

My Dad is (Awesome) *verb*
My (dad) *noun* is (awesome...) *verb*
(He) works as hard as a lawyer...
and he can (read) *verb* very very fast...
and he is (strong) *very* as a (gorilla)... *noun*
and he helps me with my (homework) *noun* when ever I need him too
(He) is good at (buildin) *verb* things... too!
(My) dad is the (greatest) *verb* one in the whole whide (world) and the best of all the rest!

She proceeds to third grade with increased ability and love for reading and writing, ready for new challenges.

■ Summaries of Three Students

Let's look now in a more general way at the accomplishments of a few other children who varied widely in ability. These samples include the work of Brett, who may have been characterized as a struggling reader; Jennifer, who started the year with more skills; and Ashley, who came to me already possessing strategies that put her beyond the stage of development of many other students. I hope you will gain a perspective on how the analogy strategies can help advance the reading and writing work of students at all ability levels.

Brett began the year really struggling as a reader and writer. The results of his reading inventory indicated that his instructional reading level was at the primer level. He struggled very deliberately to sound out every letter of every word. He tried several sounds for letters, searching for a sound that would connect with other sounds to produce a meaningful word. For example, when sounding out the word *good* on the primer word list, he tried two sounds for the letter *g* (|*g*| as in *get* and |*g*| as in *giraffe*) and several sounds for the vowel digraph *oo,* including the long and short *o* sounds. Although |*d*| did not give him much trouble, he was unable to put the one phoneme he identified together with the other sounds he was experimenting with to make a word. He seemed to have a good knowledge of individual letter-sounds; after all, he tried different sounds when attacking words, but blending those sounds was a real problem. On the word list, he was unable to read words like *away, white, his, again,* and *gobble.* It was painful to watch his slow, one-sided attempts. In the primer passage, his inefficient sounding-out strategy caused him to make miscues that didn't make sense in terms of the story. He wasn't attending to meaning and structure cues. After leaving the class for resource help in September and returning in mid-November, he was retested. He showed only slight improvement in reading skill, testing just above where he was at the first of the year but still well below first-grade level.

When Brett returned, it was difficult to help him break this habit because he was so entrenched in the single strategy of sounding out letter by letter. I concentrated on showing him the value of semantic and syntactic cues to help him balance his one-track use of graphophonic cues. He also received instruction in the analogy strategies. It took a bit longer to see the effects of this instruction with Brett, but changes did happen. Through continuous modeling, he slowly began to break his habits. By February he had advanced to the second-grade instructional level. His miscues showed evidence of attention to onset and rime. On the second-grade word list he read *el ep ant* for *elephant,* breaking the word down into chunks, although having trouble with the *ph* digraph. He also read *pic ters* for *pictures.* Context would have certainly helped him with these words. Brett was also integrating other strategies into his reading process, self-correcting errors so

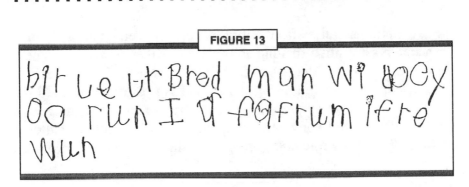

FIGURE 13

words made sense. Brett's parents remarked, "He seems to read faster and smoother, and he tries to (identify) bigger words." By the end of the school year, he was reading quite well on the second-grade level.

In writing, Brett made larger gains in less time. Figure 13 shows a sample of his writing from the first week of school. His inventive spellings included *bir* for *dear, jejr* for *ginger,* and *l a* for *away.* During class sharing time in Writing Workshop, Brett was often unable to reread his own writing for class response without my assistance. Nevertheless, he continuously volunteered to share because he was genuinely excited about what he had written. Brett made incredible gains after becoming familiar with the kinds of patterns that appear in real words. When he coupled this knowledge with listening for the chunks in words, the readability of his invented spellings dramatically improved. He was then able to proudly read his own work independently.

FIGURE 14

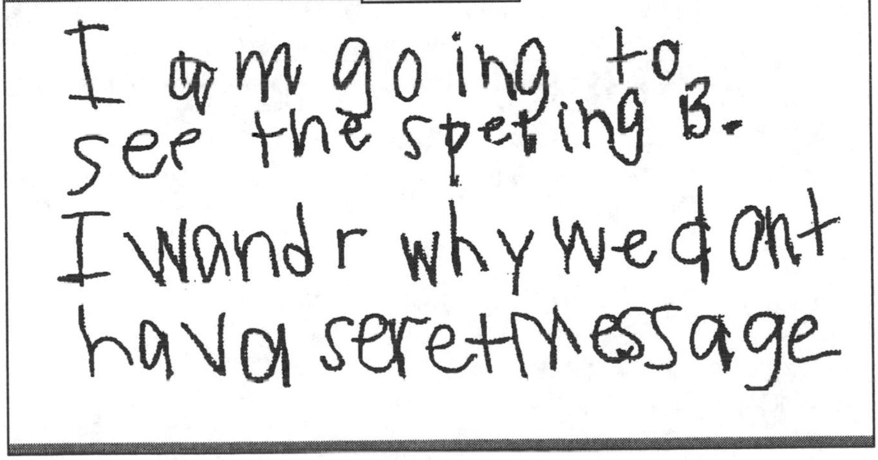

> I am going to
> see the speting B.
> I wandr why we dont
> hava seret message

Two journal entries from February (fig. 14) demonstrate the difference in his inventive spelling ability. He was then more able to hear the chunks in words than seemed to be the case in September. He wrote *speling* for *spelling* using the *ell* and *ing* patterns. He used the *et* pattern to write *seret*, producing a close approximation to *secret*. In addition, Brett used conventional spellings, which include patterns from the Wall. He wrote *am; going*, using the *o* (as in our Word Wall

FIGURE 15

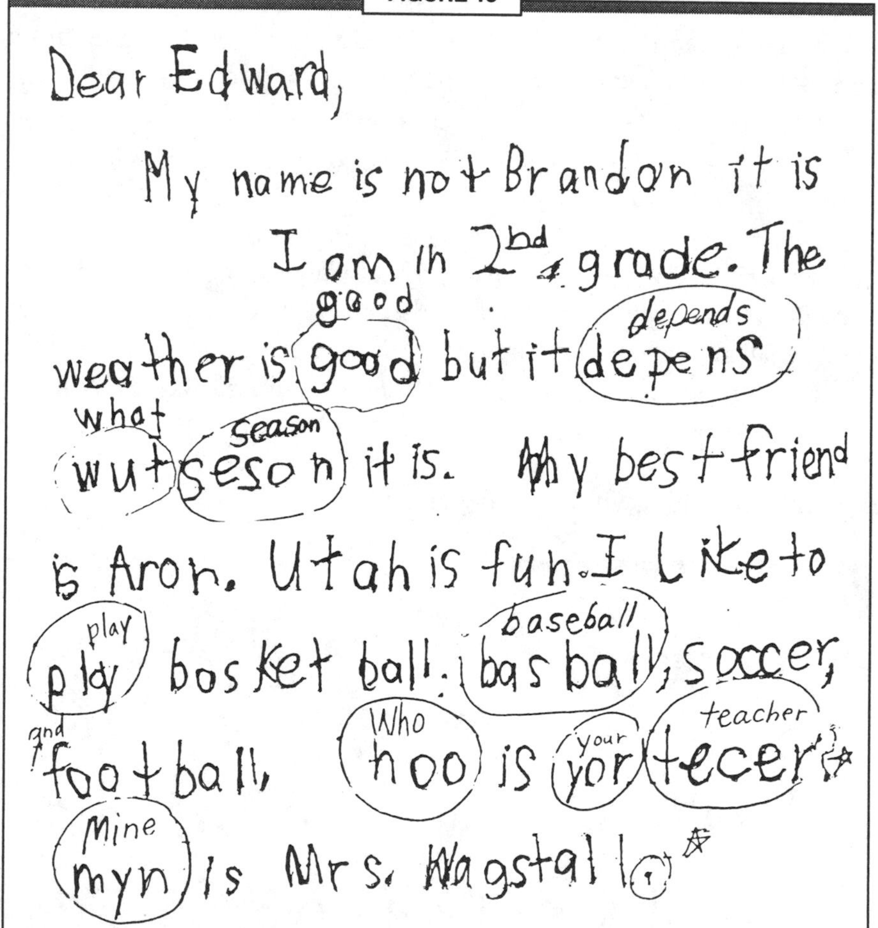

Dear Edward,

My name is not Brandon it is
I am in 2ⁿᵈ grade. The
weather is good (good) but it depens (depends)
wut (what) (seson) (season) it is. My best friend
is Aron. Utah is fun. I Like to
ply (play) bosket ball. bas ball (baseball), soccer,
and football, hoo (Who) is yor (your) tecer (teacher)
myn (Mine) Is Mrs. Wagstall.

Your friend;

word *Flo)* and *ing* patterns; and *see,* which has the *ee* pattern. Two common patterns appear in the word *message—ess* and *age.* Brett showed pattern use in Challenge Word activities as well, as when he wrote *stoopendus* for *stupendous.* I was so proud of Brett's accomplishments at this point. Instead of struggling to record every individual sound, just as he had struggled to decode small units, he was now writing more fluidly. He was gaining real confidence in writing and was constructing passages with greater ease.

His May sample utterly amazes me. I have never before seen such dramatic writing improvement over the span of one year. This penpal letter shows apparent mastery and application of many patterns in inventive and conventional spellings (see fig. 15). Invented spellings are much more logical than the attempts he made in September. He recorded *depens* for *depends, seson* for *season, wut* for *what, hoo* for *who, yor* or *your,* and *tecer* for *teacher.* This sample is 83 percent conventional. He is still acquiring correct spellings for some common glue words, and if I continued to work with Brett, I would watch closely to assure poor habits did not develop. Brett became able to effectively communicate his thoughts on paper without the guidance of an adult. The same writing progress is evident in his learning log, journal, reading response log, and Writing Workshop compositions. It was thrilling to see this budding author gain the ability to confidently share his work with the class.

JENNIFER

In September, Jennifer was reading at beginning second-grade instructional level. Her strategies were characterized by sampling letter sounds and predicting, combined with a knowledge of sight words. She refused to even attempt some of the words on the first- and second-grade lists (such as *tomorrow).* She already possessed behaviors of self-checking meaning, as shown by her ability to reread and correct miscues in the first-grade inventory passage. However, I knew her approach to using phonetic cues could be refined, thus enabling her to better balance her strategies for attacking text.

By February, Jennifer was reading at the fourth-grade level. Miscues from the fourth-grade word list show how she was attending to onset and rime. She read *a n chored* (as in *chore)* for *anchored* and *clockpit* for *cockpit.* She breezed through the lower grade lists, pausing to note the chunks in words not immediately recognized. I heard her sound words according to rime units. For instance, she read *plan et, r e pair ing,* and *inn keep er,* voicing a slight pause between each chunk. She had only four miscues on the fourth-grade passage, indicating an independent level of reading. Obviously, her ability to use context was enabling her to do very well in connected text. Her comprehension was great, and her enthusiasm for reading was skyrocketing.

It was around this time that I noticed Jennifer's newfound confidence in reading and sharing advanced texts. In my observational records, I noted that she was fascinated with the work of Roald Dahl and had begun reading many of his novels outside class. She brought them in for book share and would proudly report to me before sharing with the class. She read *The Magic Finger* and *The Enormous Crocodile* over a period of just a few evenings. We had informal discussions about these books, and I was pleased with the comments she made about things she liked in Roald Dahl's writing and connections she made with other books, events, and characters. I delighted most in sharing two things with Jennifer: first, the excitement in her accomplishments as a reader, and second, the pleasure of the wonderful stories in these great books.

Of course, now that Jennifer was energizing herself as a reader, her progress continued. In May she read the words on the fourth-grade list fluently and smoothly. She used patterns to accurately decode more advanced words on the fifth- and sixth-grade lists. I asked her to show me how she had decoded the word *hesitated,* as she had paused on this word from the sixth-grade list. She told me she knew *hes* and *it* and saw *ate* like *gate,* so she knew the word was *hesitated.* Again, her miscues showed the use of patterns. She read *con ser va ta tion* for *conservation,* mistakingly adding a chunk as she attacked the word unit by unit. Her reading of the sixth-grade passage was not marred by errors that denied meaning such as that one. The five errors she made placed her at the sixth-grade instructional level.

I interviewed Jennifer in May about her strategy use. I asked her, "What is the first thing you try when you come to a word you can't figure out from the other words in the story?" She said, "I look for the

FIGURE 16

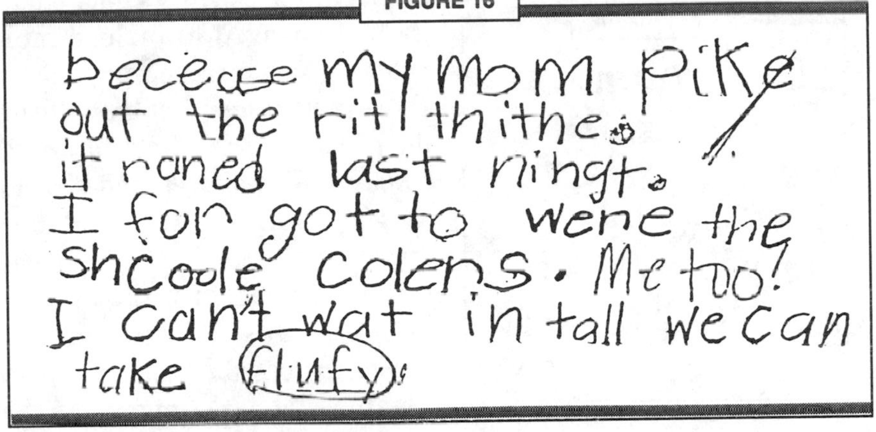

becease my mom pike
out the rit thithe.
it raned last nihgt.
I for got to wene the
shcoole colens. Me too!
I can't wat in tall we can
take fluffy.

chunks." Like the other students who were interviewed, she reported that using chunks made reading easier for her, made sense, and helped her to be a better reader.

Jennifer made similar jumps in ability and confidence in writing. Most of her early invented spellings were not characterized by the use of patterns. In a September journal entry, she wrote *pike* for *picked, rit* for *right, thithe* for *thing,* and *raned* for *rained* (see fig. 16). By December,

FIGURE 17

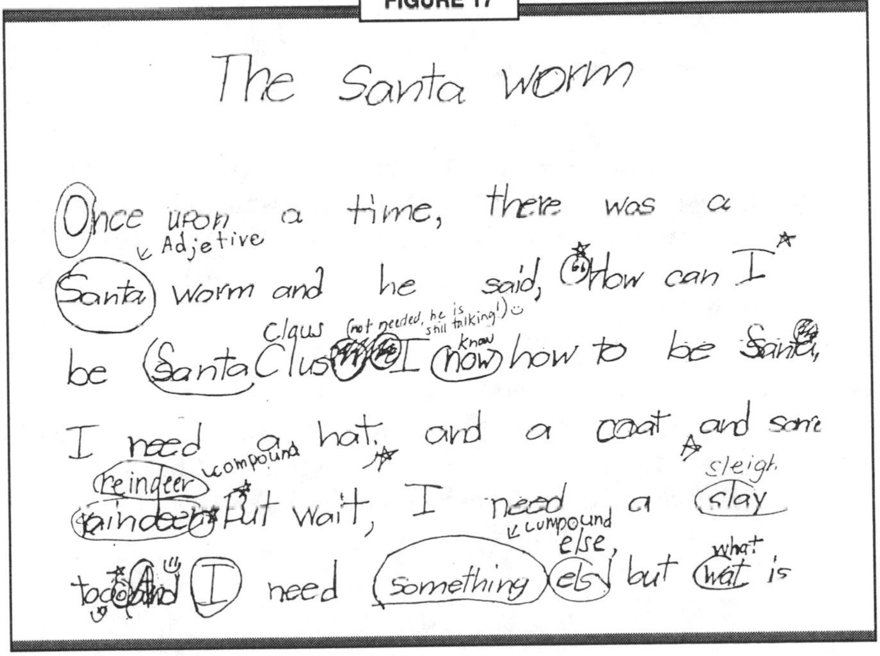

The Santa worm

Once upon a time, there was a
Santa worm and he said, "How can I
be Santa Clus? I now how to be Santa,
I need a hat, and a coat and some
reindeer. But wait, I need a slay
to. And I need something els, but what is

> **FIGURE 18**
>
> I'm going to do a book called I can't do anything with a loose tooth Lore
>
> We went on a bike ride and we went to the ice cream shop on are bikes

Jennifer's inventive spelling strategy had changed to include more patterns. While composing a story, she recorded *now* for *know* (using the pattern in *snow* from the Wall), *raindeer* for *reindeer,* and *slay* for *sleigh* (see figure 17). Her spelling strategies were in the midst of development. Thus, she attained mixed results including logical inventions based on patterns (those described above), inventions that may have been created with a more like-sounding pattern (i.e., *Clus* for *Claus* may have been invented *Claws,* and *wat* for *what* may have been inventively spelled *wut,* although it is a glue word), and conventional spellings with patterns (For example, she correctly used *ime* in *time, eed* in *need, oat* in *coat,* and *ing* in *something*). While her September sample was only 56 percent accurate, the later sample improved to 91 percent conventional spelling.

By the end of the school year, Jennifer had become a very conventional speller (see fig. 18). Many of the words included in her journal entry have patterns on the Wall. For example, she correctly used *eam* in *cream, ent* in *went,* and *ide* in *ride.* She may have even been attending to and using less frequent patterns not contained on the Wall, like *oose* in *loose* and *ooth* in *tooth.* In other May samples she is not as accurate as she is here. However, she invents spellings for very few words, using the analogy strategy when appropriate (as when she writes *gimnastic* for *gymnastics*). Jennifer wrote prolifically, sharing her work enthusiastically as she did with reading.

Ashley, an advanced student from day one, was reading at the independent level on third-grade midyear material on the September reading inventory. She was using letter-by-letter decoding to sound out unknown and difficult words. These, of course, were the strategies she

---

FIGURE 19

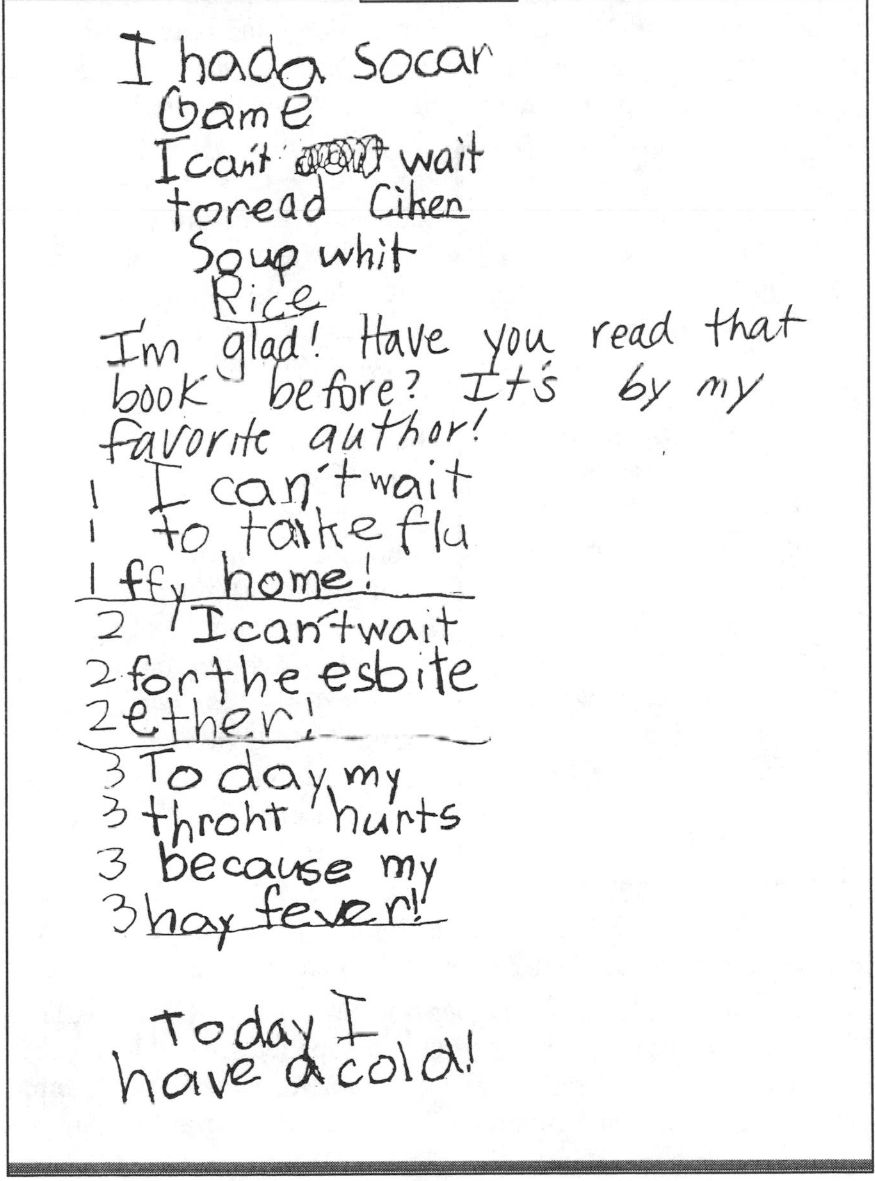

I hada socar
Game
I can't wait
to read Ciken
Soup whit
Rice
I'm glad! Have you read that
book before? It's by my
favorite author!
1 I can't wait
1 to take flu
1 ffy home!
2 I can't wait
2 for the esbite
2 ether!
3 Today my
3 throht hurts
3 because my
3 hay fever!

Today I
have a cold!

had been previously taught. She was unable to read words from the fourth-grade list like *battleground, fluttering, distance, cockpit, structure,* and *candidates.*

When I retested Ashley for the second and final time in January, she had taken off. She read the sixth-grade selection fluently, expressively, and with ease, making zero errors! Her comprehension was fabulous. Miscues from the seventh-grade word list (now, in January, her instructional level) showed her use of analogy and attention to rimes for decoding. She read *polic ticks* for *politics* and *e deal ist* for *idealist.* If these words had been embedded in context, as they are in real reading situations, Ashley might not have made those errors. She read correctly from the eighth-grade word list as well. Some examples include: *suburban, functional, individual, fortnight,* and *complained.* She showed evidence of attending to chunks, as when she broke down *exhibited* into pieces (*ex hib it ted*) while decoding it. She found other multisyllabic words, like *indicate* (from the seventh-grade list) to be equally simple. For this word she explained, "I saw *in* like *pin, dic* sorta' like *ick,* and *ate* like *gate.*" Do the analogy strategies help advanced readers? Look at the evidence and be the judge. By third term, she was bringing in novels like those from *The Boxcar Children* series by Gertrude Chandler Warner to share during book share, whereas in September, she was reading shorter, easier picture books.

> **I**n December Ashley's mother remarked, "When we go to the library, she is picking longer books, chapter books. She is looking for a challenge. She loves reading. She has an excitement about it that is different from before. I often find her in her room at her desk with a book. She will come out and say, 'Listen to this,' and then read me something and explain why she likes it. She has greater confidence than before."

Examine Ashley's September writing samples (fig. 19). These are short journal entries. Notice how she spelled *assembly* as *esbile, throat* as *throht, ciken* for *chicken* and *whit* for *with.* In a September learning log entry, she inventively spelled *dangerous* as *dangres, tomorrow* as *towwmow,* and *until* as *intale.* She was already making good attempts. However, I observed a real transformation in the way Ashley attempted to spell those creative words she longed to use. She began using analogy, and gained mastery over many patterns. As with the previous student examples, her spelling became easier to decipher while use of conventional spellings for more difficult words increased substantially. Ashley's writing samples also grew longer and longer.

Figure 20 is a letter Ashley wrote to a prominent businessman in our community in an April Writing Workshop. If you read the letter, you will really get a kick out of its contents. Additionally, note her colorful word choices and the method she used to spell those words. *Ridiculous* was spelled *rediculous,* and *situation* was encoded with spaces between the syllables as *sit chew a tion.* Ashley knew when to use analogy (for such difficult and unusual words), while conventionally spelling most other more frequent words made up of easier patterns, like *wouldn't, practice, talent, baseball, players,* and *questions.*

Through analogy, Ashley has access to many more words. If my program only focused on conventional spelling, students might not attempt to use the range of their vocabularies in their writing. As you can see, that would be very unfortunate.

■ Whole Class Progress

In all honesty, each student could represent a success story. This is evident in the overall gains made by my entire class of students at the midyear point. In September, the reading level of students ranged from first grade to mid-fourth grade (Brett was not included in this data set since he was out of the room for a few months during this period). As assessed during the first weeks of school, the average reading level of the group was second grade. By the middle of the school year, the class reading level ranged from third grade to mid-sixth grade.

FIGURE 20

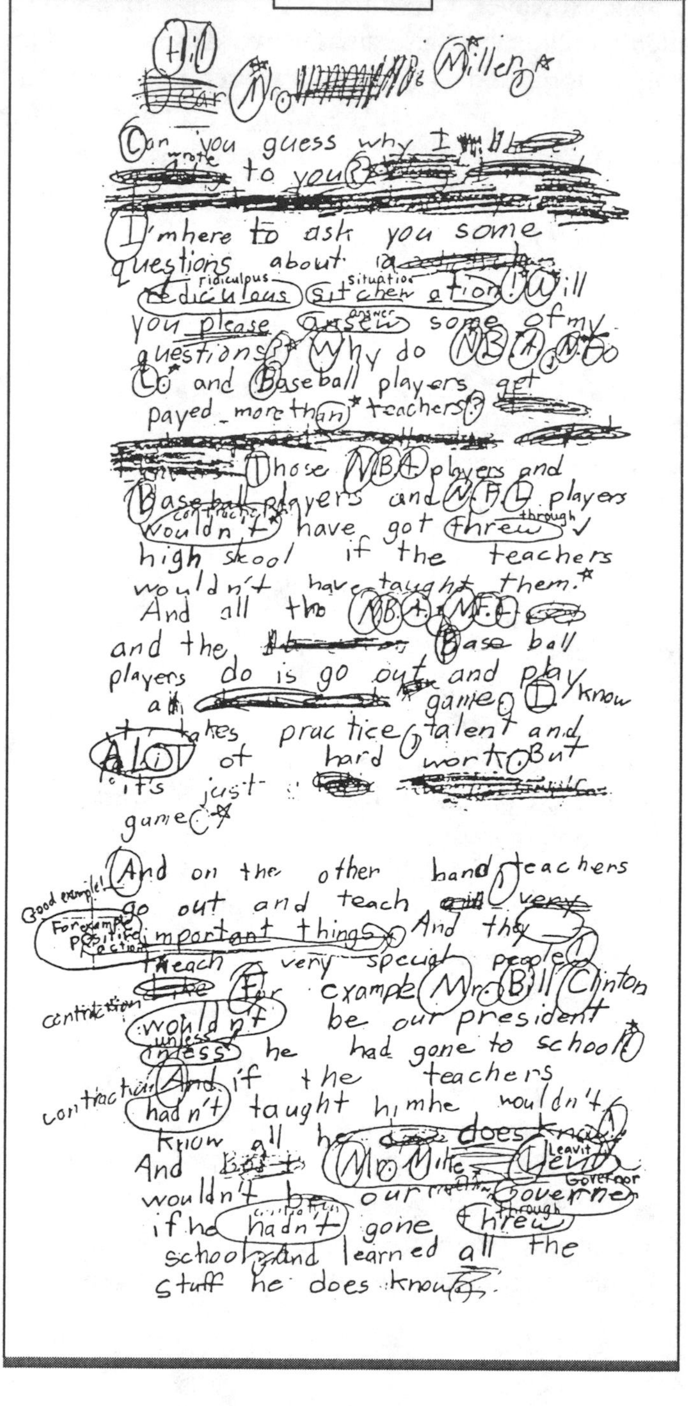

Hi!

Dear ~~Mr~~ Mr. Miller

Can you guess why I ~~wrote to you~~

I'm here to ask you some questions about a ridiculus (*ridiculus*) sichewation (*situation*) Will you plsase ansew (*answer*) some of my questions? Why do NBA, NFL Co and Baseball players get payed more than teachers?

Those NBA players and baseball players and NFL players wouldn't (*contractions*) have got threw (*through*) high skool if the teachers wouldn't have taught them. And all the NBA, NFL and the base ball players do is go out and play a game. I know it takes practice, talent and A LoT of hard work. But it's just a game.

(*Good example!*) And on the other hand teachers go out and teach ~~all~~ very (*For example* / *positive feeling*) important things. And they teach very special people. (*contractions*) For example Mr. Bill Clinton wouldn't be our president unless he had gone to school. (*contractions*) And if the teachers hadn't taught him he wouldn't know all he does know. And Mrs. Millie (*leave it*) wouldn't be our (*governor*) if he hadn't gone threw (*through*) school and learned all the stuff he does know.

As a group, they showed an average gain of 2.9 book levels over a four-month period. I regret that I was unable to retest every student at the end of the year to evaluate our total class progress. Students continued to advance, and positive reports from parents flowed in all year.

■ Looking Back

I've thought a great deal about the progress made last year. I was never before able to help my students achieve such wonderful growth even though I sincerely longed to do so. In the past, I made major modifications to my language arts program, searching for methods that worked for students. But, not until this year, with the addition of the

analogy strategies and work toward pattern automaticity, have my students truly made the gains they are capable of. This, of course, was not an experimental study with a control group. Therefore, progress cannot scientifically be linked to the analogy activities. However, I suspect analogy instruction provided the means for more productive learning than ever before. Gains were made by everyone, and evidence of growth appeared quickly. I began teaching and modeling the analogy strategies the first week of school, and I could not believe how quickly these ideas took hold. It was as if lights went on in my students' heads. Parents immediately noticed changes in the ability of their children at home. Students were not only reading and writing more, but they were doing better at these tasks. Just after the school year began, John's mother remarked, "What are you doing? I can understand what John is writing!"

I realize the whole program, with its priority for authentic literacy experiences and its integration of many reading and writing strategies, is responsible for the students' progress. But I've watched closely, noticing several fascinating behaviors that indicate students' continual reliance on the analogy strategies and control over patterns. I witnessed the way they chunk unknown words as they read and write, pausing between syllables and referring to other words. They freely talk about the words they know and how they use parts of these words. When they work cooperatively to solve reading and writing problems, they look or listen for chunks and search for analogous words together. These are the strategies students speak about in my classroom. They have friendly terms to use that make sense to them (such as "the Word Wall," "chunks," and "patterns"), and the strategies and pattern knowledge provide them with easier access to reading and writing.

Sucher, F. & Allred, R. (1981). The New Sucher-Allred Reading Placement Inventory. New York: Macmillan McGraw Hill.

6

Reflections

■ A Literate Community

My students have truly bonded as a literate community through our daily reading, writing, and sharing. Our classroom atmosphere is greatly affected by mutual respect and openness. I share my life as I write with my students. During modeled writing, they learn about my husband, my cats, my childhood, and my goals and aspirations. My students know me and I know them. I share my successes and my failures. I offer my work to them for response and genuinely consider their ideas. In the midst of one modeled writing experience, a student showed me how my title became inconsistent with the direction taken in my piece. I immediately made a change to correct this error in logic. What a great lesson, for the class, and for me! Students saw how helpful response from others can be and how I respect their input. I realized how they can do amazing things when given real opportunities.

Once the analogy strategies were part of the daily curriculum, our community of learners became tied together in yet other ways. Now students often take on a teacher role, thinking aloud about using analogies as they assist others or share their strategies. The difference between these cooperative pursuits and the kind of helping I observed in the past is that the analogy strategies allow students to aid each other both efficiently and successfully. Again, the user-friendly language and the basic sense of the strategy make this possible. I was privy to a conversation one day between Hillary and Jennifer that illustrates this point. Hillary was assisting Jennifer with inventing a spelling in a story she was composing during Writing Workshop. She said,

> "Listen for the chunks. Let's see. First we hear *po*. It's *o* like in *Flo*. So that must be *p–o*. Then we hear *tion* like in the Word Wall word *lotion,* so that must be *t-i-o-n*. It must be spelled *p-o-t-i-o-n.*"

The girls took pride in the fact they solved this writing problem independently. I was surprised at the speed and accuracy of their interaction. I knew analogy instruction was truly benefiting my students.

■ Attitudes toward Reading and Writing

With increased reading and writing skills and additional strategies for solving problems, students exude new confidence. They become as sure of themselves as Hillary was above. They know how to apply the analogy strategies quickly, independently, and they experience success. Additionally, they have a variety of real-world strategies to rely on when they are not satisfied with their attempts.

My students have an enhanced love and excitement for reading and writing. Like the examples given in Jennifer's and Ashley's profiles, students become so successful that they take on new self-generated directions. They seek new authors and more challenging books, reading more material in a shorter amount of time. They come to school eager to share. Their parents note that they spend more quality time at home on reading and writing activities.

I truly believe that the new strategies and automaticity with patterns my students now have allow them greater enjoyment of reading and writing. As readers, efficient decoding strategies combined with cues from other systems get students to the story faster than if they are struggling to solve reading problems. Quicker access to meaning allows students to enjoy the story more. As writers, effective inventive spelling techniques help them compose with greater efficiency, thus allowing them to concentrate on the substance of their stories rather than on getting sounds down on paper. Their inventive spellings improve, and in turn their ideas are better conveyed and more easily shared. Communication in writing is, of course, essential, and sharing is part of the pleasure of composing.

Naturally, our immersion in reading and writing is at the heart of these positive feelings and attitudes. The great stories in children's literature intrinsically delight us all. In my view, the analogy strategies and control of patterns have helped my students struggle less and enjoy the rewards of reading and writing more.

■ Questions and Concerns

As I brought the onset and rime theory and the analogy approaches into my classroom, several issues emerged, which I'd like to address here. These may be concerns or questions you have had while reading this book or will have when applying the techniques.

Are too few patterns learned each week?

When I began the school year adding five words to the Word Wall each week, I was concerned that the time it took to build the Wall was too great. I wondered, how can my students apply analogy if so few patterns are on the Wall? Of course, after reading this book, you may already know the answer to this question. Students enter the classroom with a variety of different abilities. Some have large sight word vocabularies already in memory, while others may know fewer words. Decoding and spelling by analogy are in fact *strategies* that students can apply by using words from their head or any other source available. So, the number of words on the Wall is not as important as it may seem.

As with Ashley, some students might only need to be directed toward focusing on the patterns in words in order to use the knowledge they already have to spell and read unknown words with greater ease and success. For some, the strategy itself is all they need and "the light goes on." They apply previous knowledge and begin self-discovering analogies in addition to the new patterns they are exposed to during instruction. Other students need more help in gaining access to patterns and developing automaticity with those chunks. That is where the Minilessons and the Word Wall come in. Actually, numerous patterns are discussed by the class throughout the week as we explore sounds and spellings in all activities. We are always looking for and evaluating patterns. Thus, students are exposed to many more than five patterns per week.

Are students overly dependent on the Word Wall?

No. The Word Wall is only one reference, and it is not the strategies themselves. During instruction, the strategy of attending to patterns (rather than individual letters) and using known words to read and write must be emphasized. Students need to understand how their own memory store and any other source can be helpful to them. I emphasized this last year, and the result was that students were not overly dependent on the Wall. They used it when they needed it. Only when they were unsure of the spelling or sound of a pattern, and absolutely needed help, did they take the time to look there. After all, I always stress quickness and fluency. Understanding and enjoying stories and getting our ideas down on paper efficiently are always main goals. Too much reliance on the Wall slows down these processes and diminishes true independence. That is why I work so hard to help students develop automaticity with patterns. Even advanced children can benefit from becoming more automatic and learning about the true nature of real patterns in our language.

Again, fluent readers decode automatically. Knowledge of patterns and the decoding by analogy strategy are tools that effectively help students to first *learn* to decode, then *master* that code through an abundance of reading and writing. The Minilessons coupled with real reading and writing build fast familiarity, recognition, and fluency with a multitude of words. I want my students to develop such fluency and use the strategies only when needed, just as adults do. I am convinced the analogy strategy is a better, more efficient, and logical way to help readers master the code faster than letter-by-letter decoding or unbalanced reliance on other cues.

In answer to the objections that few patterns are learned per week and students may become dependent on the Word Wall, I would respond that the analogy strategies may in fact be self-generating. I have alluded to this point before. As students read and write, they encounter and attend to more new patterns. When they use analogy and context to decode and listen for chunks and apply analogy to encode, they manipulate patterns, learning from experience. Their experiences expand their knowledge of patterns. Thus, students are not limited to learned or frequent patterns or references. Instead, once students attend to patterns in print, they discover analogies.

Does analogy work with words containing infrequent or irregular rimes?

Another concern is that some words in our language do not lend themselves as nicely to decoding by analogy as others. The patterns they contain are very uncommon or they have variable sounds. We've already discussed such patterns, and I've found this is not an issue that negates the credibility of this approach. As mentioned, it's relatively easy to develop automaticity with sight words that may present problems for analogy or pattern users. With multisyllabic words, recognition of a few patterns combined with context clues is fast, efficient, and very successful.

Let's look at an example and examine the possibilities. Consider the word *paragraph*. A second grader might decode *par* like *far, ag* like *rag* (or, if correctly broken into syllables, |a| like *apple),* and get stuck not recognizing the *aph* pattern or be unable to find an analogous word for that rime. The reality of authentic reading is that we usually have a context. So, if the student had *parag* (even though the sound is distorted if decoded as described above) plus a familiar context, the word would likely be revealed. The already blended sound, though distorted, gets the reader closer to the real word than letter-by-letter decoding. When these blended sounds (even in cases of distortion) are combined with other cues, the reader finds quick success. If students read on after a distorted pronunciation, I give them time to self-correct the error before asking, "Does that make sense?" or, "Would you say that? What could the word be?" Such questions cue readers to attend to meaning and often prompt students to correct their own errors.

Now, imagine the word is not in the reader's speaking vocabulary so even though the context is rich and a portion of the word has been decoded *(parag),* the word is not recognized. Here the strategies of skipping or substituting a word that makes sense become helpful. If the meaning of the passage is maintained, the reader can proceed. The real reason for reading is to make meaning. So if these strategies work, in this case, they should be tried. Of course, these are not the best strategies for attacking text because if too many words are skipped, meaning is lost. Over time as the student reads more, seeing the word in many varied contexts, and gaining more background experience, the word *paragraph* becomes automatically recognized.

From an instructional point of view, if a student struggles to decode the word *paragraph* and the context is not at all familiar, subbing or skipping won't work either because meaning can't be used to discover a like term. Picture cues could provide assistance, although it seems unlikely they would be available with this example. But, probably in this case, given the advanced nature of the word and the foreign context, the passage is beyond the instructional level and would be inappropriate for use in teaching. If a student wanted to read and find out about a new topic but was struggling with the difficulty of the text, the book could be read chorally or as a read-aloud.

This example demonstrates the importance of showing students how to integrate all strategies to be successful readers. I would not say decoding by analogy is only effective for 80 percent of words or only for words with common patterns. Instead, if the passage is instructionally appropriate and the reader has fluency with basic sight words, analogy will be effective for decoding unknown words when combined with meaning cues. Analogy provides access to many words in harder texts, more than letter-by-letter strategies, and when combined with the integrated use of all available cues, it is really powerful. You can test this assertion. If you start looking at texts and thinking about the word patterns that appear, you will find most words have patterns that can be identified easily, especially with the help of context. When you examine the type of texts you read with developing readers, you will see patterns are very consistent.

How much class time should be devoted to reading and writing?

A multitude of reading and writing experiences combined with integrated strategies work together to produce a program that makes sense and is successful. You might wonder how much time this requires daily. Looking back at our typical schedule, you see my students and I spend all morning engaged in language arts activities. Often when I share my daily plan with other teachers, they challenge how realistic it is to commit so much time to reading and writing when the curriculum is packed with too many things to teach. I do try to integrate as much as possible, bringing in books on topics students are interested in so that learning about broad subjects can occur during our morning sessions. But, more importantly, because I teach second grade and work with many developing readers and writers, I cannot do anything but devote our time to supporting them as they develop these critical skills. If they move on without being well on their way to reading and writing when they leave me, they will undoubtedly encounter trouble in the grades ahead. In the upper grades, teachers are helping students read to learn, not learn to read. They are expected to have a basic mastery of reading and writing, although we all know students continue to develop and refine their skills as they proceed. If you feel time is a problem, consider the case of New Zealand. This country was ranked best in reading education in the world by *Newsweek* (1991). Students there score at the top of international literacy tests. Fifty percent of all class time for developing readers and writers is routinely devoted solely to language arts. Time devoted to the subject is described as key to the success of New Zealand's reading program.

■ A Final Concern: Standardized Testing

I know the analogy strategies approach is backed by research, practice in the classroom, and genuine student achievement: It works! But the school system is slow to change. One concern I have centers around the nature of standardized tests. In the reading component of our district end-of-level test, students are asked to match isolated vowel sounds. A typical test item would be: given the word *seen,* which word has the same vowel sound: *treat, wed, gotten,* or *excite?* Not only do these questions not match what the research says is appropriate for developing readers, but such items focus on only small, isolated parts of words. Good readers do not focus their attention at this level once automaticity has developed. The items yield information of little importance when evaluating reading skill and strategy use. Scoring information is given in such categories as: vowel digraphs, long vowels, and short vowels. If students are trained to decode vowel sounds in isolation and are assessed at this level, what does this tell us about their ability to read and comprehend connected text? Such test items certainly were not designed with a real-world view in mind. We do not concern ourselves with decoding vowel sounds in our daily lives. Instead, we are engaged in the real acts of reading and writing as whole processes. If we are going to have standardized tests, we need assessments based on authentic activities. We can only hope the tests change to match good practice and to yield helpful information for students, teachers, and parents.

Teachers have questioned how I can defend my approach to instruction given the nature of our tests. I answer by stating three things. First, I know this approach works, as evidenced by the improved reading and writing of my students. Second, decoding by analogy instruction does in fact build phonemic awareness at all levels (even at the individual phoneme level) as students develop mastery over the code in our language, and third, I will *not* teach to a test. Instead of being driven by a test, I discard practices that do not work and replace them with something that does work. I tried teaching students to read by focusing on isolated sounds, and it didn't work. It is only fair to my students, and it is only fair to me to search for something more effective. Students should be taught with methods that promote success, and I should be able to celebrate the successes my students achieve.

■ Conclusions

The analogy strategies appear to be extremely powerful when taught in an integrated fashion and applied with flexibility. Continued research may provide further compelling evidence for how this instruction improves the progress of developing readers and writers. Meanwhile, the program I have developed maximizes the teaching of effective strategies within rich reading and writing experiences. This seems to be the best of both worlds; students develop love for reading and writing while their success is bolstered through valuable training that may help them quickly master the code. In turn, they are better able to focus their attention on higher processes, such as making meaning from texts. What happens in our classrooms does not have to be an either/or proposition. Instead, we can find a middle ground, balancing different approaches to optimize all benefits.

It appears that there are two strands to successful analogy instruction—the strategies themselves and the automaticity with rime patterns. If students do not understand the strategies, they cannot use the patterns and, conversely, without quick access to patterns, they cannot efficiently apply the strategies. Some educators may be uncomfortable with the minilessons that promote automaticity with patterns or the practice sessions that focus directly on strategy application. Keep in mind that these activities may address the various learning styles of children in our classrooms. Additionally, a balanced literacy program must give due attention to basic underlying processes and all cues available to readers. I strive to give my students as many advantages as possible while keeping activities purposefully geared. If my students can benefit from pattern recognition practice, I will include it in our day. Please note how short the review activities are and weigh the benefits against the costs for students.

The whole purpose of this book has been to help students make meaning with text. After all, that is what reading and writing are. The less time spent on decoding and encoding, the better. The strategies and activities offered are designed to help students become automatic with these skills so they may be more capable of higher pursuits. It is so important to note how the analogy strategies make sense to developing readers and writers. They know when and how to apply the strategies and why they are using them. Given these understandings, students are empowered as confident, independent learners. Look at a letter I received from Ashley this summer (Fig. 22). She writes about her own use of patterns to inventively spell the word *Neosporin* independently according to the way she hears it. She is making sense of her strategy use, knowing when, why and how to apply patterns. When we can provide students with efficient, effective tools and help them make sense of their own use of strategies, we have truly remained faithful to the goal of meaning-making.

FIGURE 22

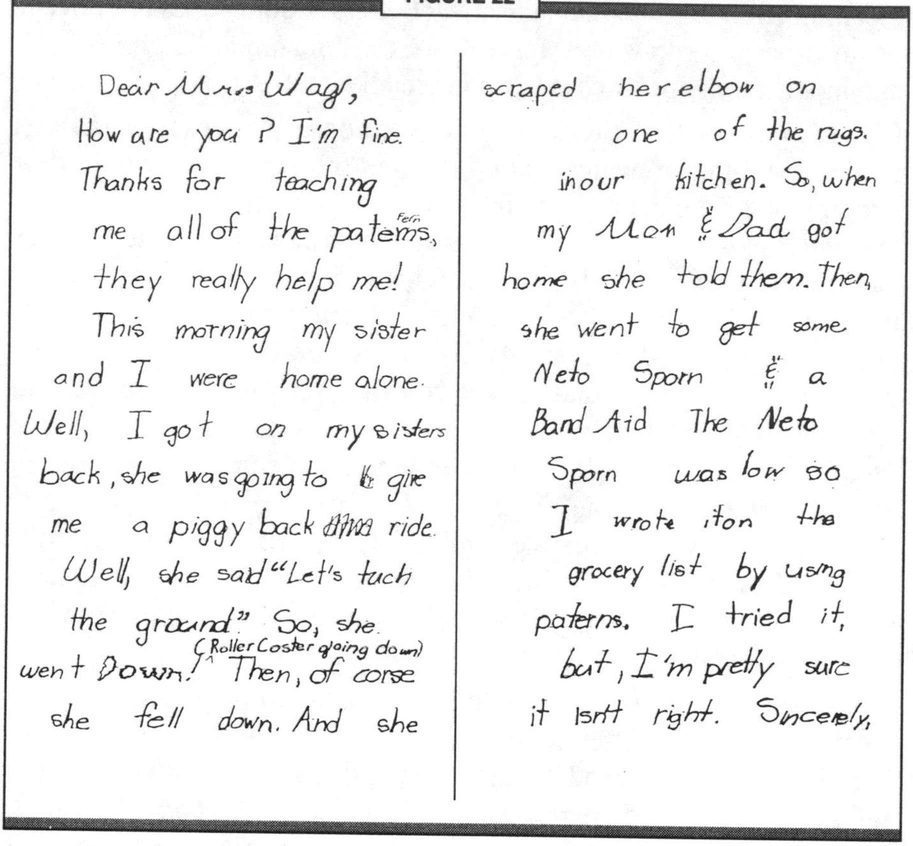

Dear Mrs Wags,
How are you? I'm fine.
Thanks for teaching
me all of the paterns,
they really help me!
This morning my sister
and I were home alone.
Well, I got on my sisters
back, she was going to give
me a piggy back ride.
Well, she said "Let's tuch
the ground." So, she
went Down! (Roller Coster going down) Then, of corse
she fell down. And she

scraped her elbow on
one of the rugs.
in our kitchen. So, when
my Mom & Dad got
home she told them. Then,
she went to get some
Neto Sporn & a
Band Aid The Neto
Sporn was low so
I wrote it on the
grocery list by using
paterns. I tried it,
but, I'm pretty sure
it isn't right. Sincerely,

Burns, B. (1991) In New Zealand, good reading and writing come
'naturally.' In The best schools in the world. Newsweek, 119, 52 (2).